The Cambridge Manuals of Science and
Literature

CASH AND CREDIT

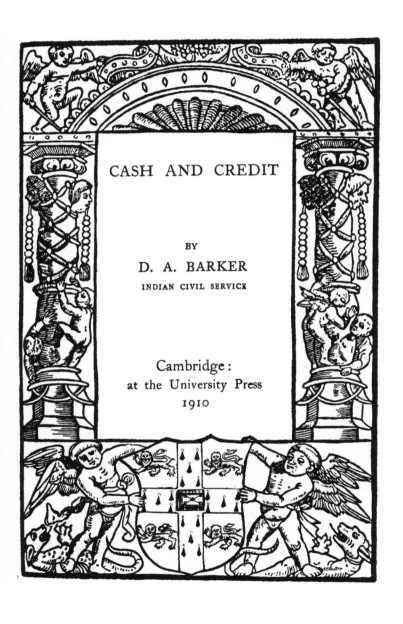

CASH AND CREDIT

BY

D. A. BARKER

INDIAN CIVIL SERVICE

Cambridge:
at the University Press
1910

CAMBRIDGE UNIVERSITY PRESS
Cambridge, New York, Melbourne, Madrid, Cape Town,
Singapore, São Paulo, Delhi, Tokyo, Mexico City

Cambridge University Press
The Edinburgh Building, Cambridge CB2 8RU, UK

Published in the United States of America by
Cambridge University Press, New York

www.cambridge.org
Information on this title: www.cambridge.org/9781107401839

© Cambridge University Press 1910

First published 1910
First paperback edition 2011

A catalogue record for this publication is available from the British Library

ISBN 978-1-107-40183-9 Paperback

Cambridge University Press has no responsibility for the persistence or
accuracy of URLs for external or third-party internet websites referred to in
this publication, and does not guarantee that any content on such websites is,
or will remain, accurate or appropriate.

With the exception of the coat of arms
at the foot, the design on the title page is a
reproduction of one used by the earliest known
Cambridge printer, John Siberch, 1521

PREFACE

THE object of this little book is to provide the reader with a stepping stone from which, fortified with a firm grasp of elementary principles, he may proceed to the study of more ambitious works. An attempt has been made to give a sketch of the theory of money in its more practical aspects, but, owing to limitations of space, many subjects of importance have been altogether omitted. No mention has been made of bi-metallism, of index numbers, of the "cost of production" theory, or, indeed, of many other questions which will be found discussed in more systematic treatises. To such treatises, therefore, the reader must go in order to complete his studies. The classic *Lombard Street* of Bagehot and Mr Hartley Wither's luminous work *The Meaning of Money* present the subject of monetary theory from the point of view of the "city man." Similar, but more technical, books are Mr George Clare's *Money Market Primer* and his *Foreign Exchanges*. *Money and Monetary Problems* by Professor Nicholson should be read by every student. The chapters devoted to bi-metallism, and other kindred subjects, in Colonel Walker's *Political Economy* are extremely lucid and will be found useful by beginners, whilst the corresponding portions of the late Professor Sidgwick's *Principles of Political Economy* afford useful examples of profound reasoning to the more advanced reader. Last, there is the monumental work of Mr Dunning Macleod—*The Theory and Practice of Banking*—which, in its historical chapters at any rate, will richly reward any reader who has leisure to attempt its perusal. To all the books mentioned the author himself has to acknowledge his indebtedness, but more particularly to the work of Mr Macleod.

SACOMBURY, WARE,
August 12, 1910.

CONTENTS

CHAPTER I

CASH AND CREDIT

WE propose, in this chapter, to take our readers to a strategic point of the modern commercial system, to the counter of a country bank, to watch with them the customers who come there to do business, and to follow out the consequences of their demands.

The first to appear is a farmer, come to cash a cheque, in order that he may be able to pay wages to his men that evening. We will suppose that it is the autumn of a year in which the harvest has been unusually good and that the demand for agricultural labour is eager. The cheque, therefore, is large, but it is only one of many that have been presented lately by the farmers of the neighbourhood. Next comes a builder. He has been employed in repairing a farm-house which, in less prosperous years, would have continued in disrepair, and he also wants some ready money for wages. Next, a shopkeeper who, under the stimulus of increased sales, wishes to start a branch in a neighbouring village, and comes to apply for a loan. Everybody seems to want ready

1

money and the manager of the bank finds his balance dwindling rapidly. Where is he to turn for money? Appeals to the other branch banks in the same neighbourhood would of course be unavailing, for *their* coffers are also becoming empty. His sole resource, therefore, is to telegraph to his London agent for such a supply of notes and cash as he requires; for it is in London that the spare money of the whole country is kept. In every civilised country there is a centre at which spare money can most advantageously be employed. To this centre, therefore, the spare money of the country will flow, and from this centre it must in any emergency be obtained. The Yorkshire farmer who draws upon his country banker really draws upon London; the Nebraska miner who sends gold to a national bank really supplies New York. The proposition which we wish to establish is this :—*More trade means a need for more money, and more money can be obtained only from the monetary centre of the country concerned.* The effects of such a withdrawal from the monetary centre will be examined at a later stage, but it will be necessary in the meantime to state more fully and to subject to certain qualifications the first half of our proposition ; that *more trade means a need for more money.*

Suppose that *A* has bought goods from *B* to the value of £100. *A* may pay *B* by giving him a hundred sovereigns, or by giving him a cheque on a banker C for £100, or by accepting a (say) three months bill of exchange for £100 drawn on him by B. In the first case, when A pays down the £100, there has been a cash payment and no credit has been given. In the second case, when A pays by cheque, there has been a cash payment but credit of a sort has been given. In the third case, where A accepts a bill of exchange, B has given three months credit to A. But the term "credit" as used in the second case bears a different meaning from that with which it is used in the third. In the second case "credit" is synonymous with confidence; in the third case "credit" implies not only confidence but also a willingness to make a loan of money. Where B accepts a cheque from A he shows his confidence in the sufficiency of A's banking account and in the solvency of his banker. Where B agrees to receive payment in the form of a three months bill of exchange accepted by A he thereby agrees to wait three months for payment (thus in reality lending £100 to A for three months) and also shows his confidence that A in three months time will be able to repay the loan. Now, if for any reason, B begins to suspect that A or his banker is likely to fail he will, as a prudent man, refuse to accept payment by cheque or by bill, and will demand the payment of one hundred sovereigns, the value of which will not be affected by any misfortune that may happen to A. But the effect of B's refusal to take a cheque may be different from the effect of his refusal to take payment by a bill of exchange. If B refuses to take a cheque A will have to pay him in gold, and thus there will be a temporary demand for one hundred sovereigns which would otherwise not have been needed. If B had not been suspicious he would have accepted A's cheque, and paid it into his bank, and there would have been no demand for money at all. But as it is, A will have to take the rejected cheque to his bank, take out gold in exchange, and pay it over to B. It is true that B may pay the gold back into the same bank almost immediately afterwards, but still for that interval the bank has been compelled to provide £100, and its position was the weaker to that extent, however short the interval might be.

If, on the other hand, B refuses to take payment in the form of a bill of exchange, not because he is suspicious of A's position, but because he is unwilling to allow A to borrow from him through the means of a deferred payment, A will be able to pay by cheque, and the demand for money is not greater than it would otherwise have been. If B, in addition to wanting immediate payment, is also suspicious of A he will demand sovereigns, and the effect, as explained above, will be a temporary demand for one hundred sovereigns which would otherwise not have been needed. We see, therefore, that a refusal to give credit, where "credit" is synonymous with confidence, has the effect of causing an increased demand for cash, but that a refusal to give "credit" where "credit" implies a loan, has no such effect.

The supply and demand for money, then, is strongly affected by changes in the state of credit or confidence. Increasing confidence will mean a less demand for money; decreasing confidence will mean a greater demand for money, quite apart from any changes in the volume of trade. And it may well be that changes in the volume of trade may be neutralised by changes in the state of credit so that increasing trade accompanied by increasing confidence, or decreasing trade accompanied by decreasing confidence, may lead to no changes in the demand for money. Our original proposition that more trade creates a need for more money, is none the less true, but it might perhaps be stated better: *Other things being equal, more trade creates a need for more money;* or else, *More trade tends to create a need for more money.*

It is sometimes objected that although this proposition may be true, that although more trade may tend to create a need for more money, yet that modern trade is carried on to such a large extent by the aid of credit instruments, such as cheques, that the increased demand for money will be of an

insignificant character. *A*, for example, buys a plot
of land from *B* and gives him a cheque in payment
which *B* pays into his bank; and the transaction is
thus completed without any demand for cash at all.
Such an example, however, is quite misleading, for it
is obvious that a trade boom is not composed entirely
of transactions such as this, but must necessarily
involve many others in which cash payments are
essential. Even if all wholesale dealings were settled
by cheque the corresponding retail transactions would
still be settled principally in cash, and wage payments
must, as a rule, be made in the same way. Under
existing conditions the use of credit instruments
applies to a certain proportion of the total number of
transactions, but that proportion will not be increased
merely because the total number of transactions
increases, and there must, therefore, under such
circumstances be a substantial demand for more
money when trade expands in volume.

*More trade, then, tends to create a need for more
money, and this money, as has been observed above,
must generally be obtained from the monetary centre
of the country concerned.* When trade is slack and
money accumulates in the coffers of the country
banker, he will send it up to London to find employment until such time as it will be wanted again in
the country. When trade is brisk the country banker
will get his supplies of gold from London to hold until

the strain is over. It is to London, also, that borrowers come to find on what terms they can borrow money. It is the equation of supply and demand in this monetary centre which we have to observe.

CHAPTER II

THE MONEY-MARKET IN THEORY

WE must now consider the nature of the business transacted by a typical banking institution situated at a monetary centre such as that described in the last chapter; and for such information we turn naturally to the balance sheets periodically issued by the bank for the benefit of the public. These balance sheets, however, contain on both sides details which are not essential to the limited scope of this chapter and which may, therefore, for our present purpose, be omitted. In its most simplified form the balance sheet may be represented as follows:

Liabilities	£	Assets	£
Deposits of customers	20,000,000	Cash	4,000,000
		Investments ...	2,000,000
		Loans to customers	14,000,000
	£20,000,000		£20,000,000

To avoid the complications which would arise if we had to consider transactions between many different banks, we will suppose that this represents

the consolidated balance sheets of all the banks at
our monetary centre; the items shown here being
simply the totals of similar items in the individual
balance sheets. The total liability of all the banks,
then, amounts to £20,000,000, and against this liability they can show £4,000,000 of actual cash,
£2,000,000 invested in securities, and £14,000,000
lent to customers.

Firstly, then, as to the item "deposits of customers."
To the average non-commercial man a bank is merely
an agency for keeping his spare cash and for collecting
the money due on cheques payable to him. For him
a "deposit" really is a deposit, and the use of such a
word naturally leads him to believe that the sum of
£20,000,000 entered under this description has actually
been deposited in the banks by their customers. But
the nature of his mistake is revealed by considering
the case of the commercial man who wishes to borrow
from a bank. This would-be borrower, we will
suppose, is an enterprising man and asks for a good
round sum, say, one million sterling; in which request the bank manager good-naturedly acquiesces.
Having obtained his loan, the borrower has to decide
what to do with it. He might, in very unusual
circumstances, ask for cash down, but, as a general
rule, the bank will give him a credit on its books,
and he will draw cheques against that credit as
necessity arises. What will be the effect of this

transaction on the balance-sheet? If he asks for cash the item "cash" will be reduced by one million sterling and the item "loans to customers" will be increased by a similar amount, thus:

Liabilities	£	Assets		£
Deposits of		Cash		3,000,000
customers	20,000,000	Investments ...		2,000,000
		Loans to customers		15,000,000
	£20,000,000			£20,000,000

But if he merely accepts a credit in the bank's books the change will be as follows:

Liabilities	£	Assets		£
Deposits of		Cash		4,000,000
customers	21,000,000	Investments ...		2,000,000
		Loans to customers		15,000,000
	£21,000,000			£21,000,000

In this latter case we see that there has been a change on both sides of the account, and that the items "deposits of customers" and "loans" have both been increased to the extent of one million pounds. This is, then, the important point, that a loan by the bank to a customer increases the item "deposits," and that "deposits" therefore are not made up, as they might seem to be, merely of idle balances and savings, but also of credits given by the bank.

But we have not yet arrived at the end of the transaction.   The borrower would not have asked for a loan unless he wished to spend the money, so we may presume that he will shortly draw cheques on the lending bank to the amount of one million pounds. In consequence of this, his credit for one million will be extinguished and the amount of "deposits of customers" *at that bank* will be reduced by a similar amount.   But if, as will very likely be the case, the cheques drawn by the borrower are payable to residents in the same monetary centre, the recipients of the cheques will send them to banks of this centre and the amount of customer's deposits at these banks will be increased by the sum of one million pounds. Considering all the banks of this centre as one we see, therefore, that the consolidated balance-sheet will still show "deposits of customers" to the amount of twenty-one million pounds.   It may be objected that some of the cheques drawn by our millionaire borrower might have been sent to persons resident in the country and paid by them into a country bank. But even then, owing to the tendency of money to collect at the monetary centre, the country banker would probably use the cheque to obtain a credit for that amount with his central agent, and the result would be the same as if the cheque had originally been paid into one of the central banks.   Even if the borrower wishes to use his credit to pay a creditor living in a foreign country he will do so by buying a bill on that country from a bill-merchant, and will pay for the bill with a cheque. The bill-merchant will pay that cheque into his banking account, and so, as before, the sum total of customers' deposits remains at the amount of twenty-one million pounds. Twist the matter as we may, the loan of one million has increased customers' deposits by an equal amount.

It would appear, then, that provided a borrower is willing to take his loan in the form of a credit on the bank's books, and provided that the person to whom he gives cheques return these cheques to a bank for collection, the process of credit-making may go on indefinitely, since its only effect is to increase the items " deposits of customers " and " loans." And since the banks benefit by the credits which they give, and the customers of the banks benefit by the credits which they get, it appears, further, that the process of credit-making would go on indefinitely unless it were stopped by some powerful and universal forces. The nature of these forces has to a certain extent been indicated by the qualifications of the above statement, but, to make the matter more clear, we will give an example of their working. For this purpose let us take the case of a very small borrower, one who is content to apply for the modest sum of £100, and let us consider how this loan will affect the banks according to the different ways in which it may be used. In practical life the ways of using money vary from expenditure on fireworks to expenditure on raw materials for the purposes of industry; but for our present purpose, fortunately enough, there is no necessity to attempt any definition of luxuries or necessaries, of investment or expenditure. It is sufficient to avoid the difficulty by taking extreme cases and neglecting all intermediate forms. As already explained the primary effect of the loan has been to increase the total of customers' deposits by £100. In the first place, then, suppose that our borrower decides to spend his money on fireworks. If he pays by cheque, and the seller of fireworks, as he probably will do, sends the cheque to his own bank, the total of customers' deposits will remain increased by an amount of £100 as in the case of the millionaire borrower. The buyer may, however, elect to draw one hundred sovereigns from his bank, and pay for the fireworks in cash. If he does this, the item "deposits of customers" will be reduced by the amount of £100 to its former level, and the item "cash" will be reduced by a similar amount. But this state of affairs will not last long. The firework seller will find money accumulating in his till, and shortly after the purchase he will send (say) £100 in cash to the bank. This will increase the items "deposits of customers" and "cash" and

the consolidated balance-sheet will finally be precisely
the same as if only cheques had passed.

But now suppose that our borrower, instead of
spending his money on luxuries, decides to use it
in engaging some labourers for the more intensive
cultivation of his farm.   He engages, then, three
labourers at thirteen shillings a week, and uses his
borrowed money to pay their wages.   In order to be
able to pay his increased wages bill he will have to
withdraw from his bank thirty-nine shillings more
than he used to do.   But at the end of the year, if he
has laid his plans well, he will find that his increased
receipts are at least sufficient to enable him to cover
the payment of interest to the bank and to continue
to employ the three extra men without borrowing
any more money.   As long as this investment of
£100 remains, three more labourers will remain
employed than there would otherwise have been, and
this extra employment leads to a greater demand for
cash.   In consequence of more earning there is more
spending; the local shops do a brisker trade and keep
a larger sum in their tills.   All this implies that the
money drawn out of the bank by means of the
borrower's cheque does not all drift back to the bank
via the pocket of the labourer and the till of the
shop ; part of it, indeed, will do so, but part will
remain in circulation, and will, to that extent,
diminish the items "deposits of customers" and

" cash." But when the loan was used to buy fireworks
we saw that neither of these items were affected.
It is the variations of the latter item which are of
greatest importance, and roughly speaking, we may
say, therefore, that *loans which are used by the
borrowers for reproductive purposes will cause a
demand for cash, while loans used merely for un-
productive expenditure will not do so.* But most
loans are used for reproductive purposes and therefore
imply a demand for cash, and it is this demand which,
as we shall see, puts a limit to that indefinite expansion of credit which otherwise would be to the
advantage of both banks and customers[1].

There is, however, another aspect of the question
to be considered. Suppose that at the end of the
year the manager of the bank considers that he is
lending too freely, and refuses to renew the loan of
£100. The farmer, if he cannot borrow from elsewhere, will be unable to continue to employ the three
extra men whom he had engaged on the strength of
the loan. Consequently his weekly wage-bill will be
decreased, and so will the taking of the shops once
patronised by the dismissed labourers. There will

[1] Another potent check to the indefinite expansion of credit will
be explained at a later stage. It lies in the action of the foreign
exchanges. An expansion of credit tends to cause a rise of prices
and so to produce an outward flow of gold. Then the bankers, in
order to maintain a proper proportion of cash to liabilities, will have
to contract their credits.

therefore be a small but definite decrease in the amount of money required for wage payments and retail transactions, and the money so displaced will drift back to swell the cash reserves of the banks at the monetary centre. Thus we reach the conclusion that a contraction of loans, in so far as it causes a contraction of trade, will tend to increase cash reserves. In this connection it is necessary to observe that a contraction of loans is sometimes spoken of as a contraction of credit; that the term "credit," as already noticed, has two meanings and that its indiscriminate use is therefore likely to cause confusion. In one case a contraction of credit means a contraction of loans, and so may be an indirect cause of increased cash reserves. In the other case a contraction of credit connotes a feeling of insecurity which may cause an unusual demand for payments in coin, and so tend to diminish the cash reserves of the bank.

The term "cash" implies actual money in the coffers of the bank. This reserve of cash is the only perfectly reliable reserve which a banker can keep. In times of acute panic he may be unable to sell his securities, and equally unable to call in his loans to customers, but the gold in his vaults cannot depreciate in value, and it cannot run away. If, therefore, we wish to get a rough indication of the financial strength of a bank we must work out the proportion of "cash" to "deposits of customers." Some banks are more cautiously conducted than others and show a higher proportion of cash to liabilities, but broadly speaking, it may be said that bankers as a body will not permit this proportion to fall below a certain figure. Loans for productive purposes, as we have explained above, necessarily imply an increased demand for cash, and this can only be obtained from the banks. But a continuous fall in the amount of cash in the banks, whether accompanied or not by a change in the amount of deposits, will rapidly reduce the proportion of cash to liabilities to a dangerously low figure, and there will be an immediate check to the extension of credit. The most daring of bankers will cease to lend when his cash reserve has shrunk beyond a certain point. On the other hand, the most cautious will increase his loans when cash becomes abundant in his vaults. Thus it becomes evident that the superstructure of credit cannot be indefinitely increased or decreased without any reference to the cash basis upon which it rests, but that, within certain broad limits which will vary with the state of credit and the general organisation of commerce, it must depend upon and vary with the size of that cash basis.

We have spoken of bankers ceasing to lend or increasing their loans, but this phraseology does not accurately represent the course of events in an actual money-market. There, a banker will rarely refuse to lend *at a price*, provided that good collateral security

were offered. On the other hand, also, a banker
cannot increase his loans independently of increased
demand unless he lowers the price, for otherwise the
borrower would refuse to borrow. The price of such
loans is called the rate of discount, or the rate of
interest, according to the form taken by the loan. In
treating of the details of the money-market, it is
necessary to differentiate between these two rates,
but for the purposes of a broad survey it is per-
missible to look to their essential similarity and to
include them under one name; say, the rate of
interest. We can now amend our former statement
and say, that *a fall in the cash reserve will cause the
bankers to raise their rate of interest while a rise in
the cash reserve will cause them to lower their rate
of interest.* But we saw, also, that an extension of
loans, if followed by an expansion of trade, will
trench upon the cash reserves, and, conversely, that
a reduction of loans (unless accompanied by a feeling
of insecurity) will cause a shrinkage of trade, and so
swell the cash reserves. Finally, combining these
two statements of cause and effect, we see how the
three factors act and react upon each other. Increased loans, followed by an expansion of trade,
drain away coin, and so lead to a rise in the rate of
interest. A rise in the rate of interest lessens the
demand for loans, discourages trade, and so tends to
drag coin back to the banks.

But there is another element in the money-market which is of great importance and which still remains to be considered. This is the general level of prices. Suppose that in an isolated community the population are exclusively employed in the manufacture of that vague but convenient commodity known as goods in general, and that by their labours they produce goods in general to the amount of X tons a year. Further, suppose that in any one year, at the then existing level of prices, the total money income of the community is £Y. Then, since, in these days, when people do not bury their gold, all income is either spent by the recipient or lent by him to be spent by others, the whole income of £Y will be offered for the whole production of X tons, and the price of goods in general will be represented by Y/X. But suppose that in the year under consideration the banks of this isolated community were to grant to their customers credits to the amount of £Z. Then the total amount of money offered for goods in general would be £$Y + Z$, and, since the amount of goods in general will be unaltered, the price will be represented by £$Y + Z/X$. It therefore becomes obvious that an increase in Z, that is an increase in the amount of loans granted by bankers, will tend to raise prices until counteracted by an increase in X, that is, an increase in the amount of goods produced. Conversely, a decrease in the amount of loans granted by bankers must tend to lower prices until the amount of goods produced is correspondingly diminished.

If, however, we suppose that our imaginary community, instead of being isolated, is connected by the closest bonds of commerce with foreign countries, then any rise in prices brought about by an increase of loans will immediately be counteracted by a great increase of imports; and an increase of loans in any one community will only raise prices in so far as it can affect prices all the world over. In the terms of our formula, X will vary with every change of Z so that $Y + Z/X$ remains practically constant; whereas when dealing with the case of an isolated community, X, the total flow of production, is a quantity not subject to great and sudden changes. In actual life a commercial community is not perfectly interconnected with foreign countries, nor is it, of course, absolutely isolated. The truth, in fact, lies somewhere between these two extremes, and we are, therefore, at liberty to say that *an increase of loans will tend to cause a rise of prices, and that a decrease of loans will tend to cause a fall of prices*, though these changes in price will not be nearly so great as would have followed upon an equal increase or decrease of loans in an isolated community.

Thus we see that the four main elements of the money-market are linked together and that a change in one gives rise to compensating movements on the part of others. An increase of loans is followed by a rise in prices; a rise in prices is followed by an expansion of trade which drains away cash from the banks, and so leads to a rise in the rate of interest. A rise in the rate of interest lessens the demand for loans, lowers prices, and discourages trade. This again leads to a return of cash to the banks, a lower rate of interest, more loans and higher prices. And so the action and reaction goes on from day to day.

CHAPTER III

THE HYDRAULIC MODEL

WE are now in a position to exemplify, by means of a mechanical model, the working of the forces which we have described in the last chapter. Suppose, then, a cylinder AB^1 open at the upper, and closed at the lower, end. This cylinder is partly filled with water, and into the upper end is inserted a closely-fitting piston-head P, so as to touch the surface of the water. To the piston-head is attached one arm of a lever, L, the other arm being attached to a spring S. The bottom of the spring is attached to one of a series of pegs, so that it exerts a certain pull on the lever and tends to raise the piston-head. If the piston-head were to rise the other arm of the lever would fall, and the pull exerted by the spring would decrease. Inside the cylinder, and immersed in the water, is an elastic bag, C, attached to a pump which passes through the side of the cylinder so that the bag can be inflated with air, or deflated from the outside. Suppose,

[1] See Fig. 1.

now, that the area of the end of the cylinder represents the volume of the internal trade of England. It is difficult to devise any mechanical contrivance whereby the cylinder might be made to grow fatter or thinner so as to represent variations in the volume of trade, but it is a difficulty which may easily be surmounted by an exercise of the imagination. Suppose, further, that the amount of water in the

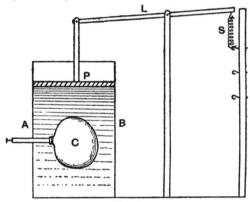

Fig. 1.

cylinder represents the amount of coin in the country, that the height of the water, and consequently of the piston-head, in the cylinder represents the level of prices, that the size of the elastic bag C represents the extent to which credit instruments are used, and that the strain on the spring S

represents the rate of interest charged by bankers for loans.

Now, supposing the model to be in a state of equilibrium, let us disturb the various forces one by one and watch the movements brought about in the different parts by such disturbance. First, then, suppose that the cylinder gets fatter, that is to say that the internal trade of the country increases. The obvious result of this will be that the level of the water falls and with it the piston-head. The far end of the lever will therefore rise, and so increase the strain on the spring. Translating these mechanical movements into the language of the market-place, we see that an increase in trade will lower the level of prices, and raise the rate of interest. If, on the other hand, the cylinder gets thinner, the piston-head will rise and the strain on the spring will decrease. Again translating, we see that a falling off in the volume of trade will be accompanied by a rise in prices and a fall in the rate of interest[1]. The practical reader may here feel inclined to point out that high prices are associated with a boom, and low prices with a slump, in trade, and that the machine is obviously mistaken. And this interruption affords a good opportunity to remind the reader that individual causes are now being isolated, and are pre-

---

[1] It must be remembered that the term "rate of interest," as used here, includes what is generally known as the rate of discount.

sumed to act while other conditions remain the same. Such a state of affairs seldom, if ever, occurs in practice, and the theoretical result, though outside our usual experience, is none the less sound. The fact is that a boom in trade is almost necessarily accompanied by an expansion of credit, and that this expansion may be sufficiently great not only to counteract the fall of prices which would be caused by an expansion of trade alone but even to send the price index substantially higher than it was before. This process may easily be followed on the model. The cylinder fattens to represent an expansion of trade, but, at the same time, we must pump air into the bag C to represent an expansion of credit. If we pump quickly enough, the expansion of the bag will more than counteract the effects of a fattening of the cylinder, the piston-head will rise, and the strain on the spring will be decreased, i.e. prices will rise and the rate of interest will fall. A period of trade depression, on the other hand, must be represented not only by a thinning of the cylinder but also by a great decrease in the size of the credit bag C; and the final result of these two may well be a fall of the piston-head and an increased strain on the spring, that is, a fall of prices and a rise of the rate of discount.

If we assume that, as the strain on the spring S increases, the girth of the cylinder will tend to diminish (just as a pull at both ends of a rubber tube will make the tube narrower); and that as the strain on the spring diminishes the girth of the cylinder will tend to increase; we obtain another analogy, viz. that a rise in the rate of interest will tend to check the expansion of trade; a fall in the rate of interest will tend to encourage it. Looking at the movements of the piston-head, we see that if other things were equal there would be a rise of prices in the first event and a fall of prices in the second. But other things will not be equal. The rise or fall of the rate of interest will be accompanied by a deflation or inflation of the credit bag sufficient not only to counteract but also to reverse the price movements which would otherwise have taken place. That is to say, a fall of prices will follow an increased rate of interest and *vice versa*.

Variations in the volume of the credit bag *C* may be ascribed to two different causes. Firstly, to changes in the extent to which book-credits, cheques and other substitutes are used in place of coin. Secondly, to changes in the amount of credit with which the banks are prepared to trust their customers. These changes tend to take place at the same time and in the same sense. Thus the same feeling of distrust which induces a man to demand payment in gold instead of by cheque will also cause the banks to be more careful as to their loans.

Similarly a feeling of confidence will encourage the use of credit instruments as well as the creation of bankers' obligations.   In times of panic or distrust, therefore, under the influence of both of these changes the credit bag will collapse, the piston-head will fall, and the strain on the spring will increase and so tend to diminish the girth of the cylinder. That is, prices will fall, and the rate of interest will rise and so discourage trading.   Conversely, in times of confidence the credit bag swells, the piston-head rises, the strain on the spring is decreased and the cylinder tends to fatten.   That is, the rate of interest falls and trading is encouraged.

CHAPTER IV

THE FOREIGN EXCHANGES IN THEORY

So far we have been considering the changes and chances of an isolated money-market which is not affected by the monetary conditions of other countries. We must now take into consideration not only the home market but also the foreign markets and the various links by which all money-markets are connected. But we will still stipulate for some limitations to the argument, and will confine it to countries which have a gold standard and which trade freely in gold. Within these limitations we may say that the adjustment of the foreign exchanges is part of the mechanism whereby the supply of gold is distributed to the various countries in accordance with their requirements. The rate of exchange itself is merely a sign of this adjustment. A flag floating in the breeze shows us which way the wind is blowing ; the rate of exchange shows us which way money is flowing or tending to flow between the various countries.

Looking at the money article of the *Times* this evening I see that the rate of exchange on Paris is quoted at 25.15. The meaning of this figure is, that any person who likes to do so can pay down one sovereign in London and acquire the right to receive 25.15 francs in Paris. Here we seem to be exchanging a gold coin in England for silver coins in Paris ; but this is not really the case. The rate is quoted in terms of smaller units merely in order to escape the awkward fractions which would result from using the large units for this purpose. In reality the exchange is one of gold coins of one weight and fineness in London for gold coins of different weights and fineness in Paris. Now it is obvious that when two coins of different weight are made of the same material, there will subsist between them a physical relation which will remain invariable under all circumstances provided that their weights are unaltered. Between the ten-shilling piece and the sovereign this relation will obviously be one-half. Between the sovereign and the napoleon it is $\frac{25.22}{20}$; and between the sovereign and the German eagle $\frac{20.42}{20}$. Since the weights of the coins are given to them at the mints, this relation is called the Mint par of exchange. Omitting in each case (as is always done in practice) the divisor 20, we may say that the Mint par of exchange is 25.22 between London and Paris, and 20.42 between London and Berlin.

Besides the Mint par of exchange there are two other rates of exchange which are of special importance. Suppose that a trader, A, were to send a hundred sovereigns to Berlin, his agent at Berlin could take them to a Berlin bank and there get an equal weight of gold in eagles; that is, $\frac{2042}{20}$ eagles. But A will have to pay the expense of insuring and shipping his hundred sovereigns from England to Germany. These expenses expressed in German currency would amount to about twelve marks[1], and therefore the net sum realised by A in Berlin is $\frac{2032}{20}$ eagles. If, on the other hand, B, in Berlin, wishes to realise 100 sovereigns in London he can take $\frac{2042}{20}$ eagles to his bank, obtain 100 sovereigns (or an equivalent weight of gold) in exchange, and ship them to London. His expenses will amount to 12 marks, so that, to get his 100 sovereigns in London, he will have to pay $\frac{2052}{20}$ eagles in Berlin. These points on the exchange schedule which are obtained by calculating the rates which would obtain on the actual shipment of gold in either direction are called the "gold points." In the German exchange, as we have shown, the gold points are 20.32 and 20.52; in the French exchange they are 25.14 and 25.30[2]. The former is the rate which is finally obtained by a resident in England who exports

---

[1] 20 marks = 1 eagle.

[2] As the expense of shipping gold varies from time to time, and from individual to individual, these figures can only be regarded as approximate.

sovereigns and turns them into eagles in Berlin or
napoleons in Paris. It is therefore known as the
"export point." The latter is the rate obtained by
one who imports eagles or napoleons and turns them
into sovereigns in London. It is known as the
"import point." The importance of the rates of
exchange known as "gold points" arises from the
fact that they represent the farthest limits between
which the rate of exchange can oscillate so long as
gold is freely forthcoming for export in both countries;
and also from the fact that any approach of the rate
of exchange to these points is a sign that gold is
tending to flow out or run in.

Suppose that any person living in London wishes
to pay a debt in Bristol, he can do so by buying a
money order at some London post office and sending
it by post to his creditor, who will be able to cash it
at a Bristol post office. Similarly if a merchant, *A*,
wishes to pay some debts in Paris he will go to an
exchange broker, buy a bill on Paris for the required
amount, and will send that to his creditor, who will
be able to cash it at his bank. But supposing that
our Londoner, on going to the post office to buy a
money order, say, for one pound, were to be told
that the commission was sixpence he would refuse
the money order, buy a registered envelope and send
the sovereign to Bristol in that. So, if the merchant
were told by the exchange broker that 100 sovereigns

would only buy a bill on Paris for 2500 francs, he would prefer to ship the sovereigns, or the corresponding amount of bullion, to Paris, and there turn it, at the Mint par of exchange, into 2522 francs, a sum which, after deducting 8 francs for freight and insurance, would leave him with 2514 instead of the 2500 francs offered by the exchange broker. It is therefore obvious that the Paris exchange can never fall below 25.14. On the other hand, it is obvious for similar reasons that the Paris exchange cannot rise above 25.30, for if the brokers were to attempt to ask for a higher rate all Paris debtors would pay their London creditors by shipping gold.

Between the two limits, the nature of which we have just explained, the rate of exchange is continually varying, and it remains for us to consider the causes which lead to these variations. In order to avoid the unnecessary and unessential complications which arise in the case of two countries having different currencies, we will revert to our former homely example of transactions between London and Bristol. These towns, we will suppose, are isolated communities trading only with each other, and conducting their exchange business through the medium of a firm, the "post office," having branches in each town. The London branch of the post office will supply money orders which may be cashed by the

Bristol branch, and the Bristol branch will similarly supply money orders which may be cashed at the London branch ; so that debtors in either town will be able to pay their foreign creditors by means of these orders. Suppose that during a certain month Bristol buys goods to the value of £100,000 from London, while London only buys £60,000 worth from Bristol. Then, if all these goods are promptly paid for, the Bristol post office will sell during the month money orders on London for £100,000, and will be asked for payment of orders sent from London to the amount of £60,000, and their balance will be increased by £40,000. Similarly the London post office will sell orders on Bristol for £60,000 and will cash orders on London for £100,000, thus diminishing their balance by £40,000. If we suppose that each of the two branches of the post office keeps its balance at a bank, the one in Bristol, the other in London, it is obvious that changes in the amount of their balances will not, of themselves, have any effect upon the money market either of Bristol or of London ; for these changes will merely take the form of a transfer of credits on the books of the bank from one customer, i.e. the post office, to other customers, i.e. those to whom the money orders are payable. But if the inhabitants of Bristol continue for any length of time to buy more from London than the inhabitants of London buy from Bristol, it may happen that the balance of the London post office will be in danger of becoming entirely exhausted. In such case the post office can add to its balances in either of the two following ways. It may deposit securities with a bank and obtain authority to overdraw, or it may request the Bristol branch of the post office to draw out in gold a portion of the superabundant balance held there, and to send this gold to London. If the first plan be adopted the total amount of credit granted by London banks will be increased by the amount of the post office overdraft. This increase of credit, as has already been shown, will tend to raise prices in London. If the second plan be adopted the stock of gold held by Bristol banks will be reduced by the amount of gold sent from Bristol to London. This will cause the Bristol bankers to contract their credits, and so tend to lower prices in Bristol. But a fall of prices in Bristol will have the same effect as a rise of prices in London, i.e. people will be encouraged to buy more in Bristol, and less in London, and thus to reverse the former balance of trade in which we supposed Bristol to buy more from London than London did from Bristol. Thus an unequal balance of trade calls into play forces which tend to correct that balance.

But the borrowing of money from a bank or the shipment of gold from one town to another is an expensive process, and the post office, therefore, tries to discourage those wishing to purchase postal orders which will render necessary such a course, and gives favourable terms to those whose purchases tend in the opposite sense. This the post office does by varying the rate of commission on money orders, that is, in other words, by varying the rate of exchange. When the balance of trade is equal between the two towns we may suppose that the post office in Bristol charges £1 0s. 1d. for a £1 money order on London, and *vice versa* ; but when Bristol begins to buy more from London than London does from Bristol, and the demand for money orders on London begins to get keen, the Bristol branch will put up its price to, say, £1 0s. 2d. If the demand still continues the price will be still further advanced, until finally (if we suppose the cost of sending £1 between London and Bristol to be 3d.) it reaches "gold point," i.e. £1 0s. 3d. If the rise in the rate of exchange to gold point does not stop the demand for money orders on London, the only course is for the Bristol post office to continue to sell orders at that rate, and to send to London the gold received in payment for these orders, and so to replenish the balances of the London post office. So long as gold is available for export from Bristol the rate of exchange cannot go beyond gold point, for if the post office were to demand more, those who had debts to pay in London would refuse to buy money orders and would discharge their debts by the alternative method of sending gold to London themselves. But the London branch can also do something to reverse the current by offering to sell money orders on Bristol at a discount, and so encouraging Londoners, by buying these money orders on Bristol, to replenish its dwindling balances. On our hypothesis it would cost the post office 3d. to bring £1 in gold from Bristol to London, and the post office will therefore be willing to sacrifice 3d. on every transaction which saves them from the necessity of such a shipment. It follows that £1 minus 3d., or 19s. 9d., will, under such circumstances, be the price of an order on Bristol. Here, too, the rate of exchange has reached gold point, but here it is the "import point," whereas in Bristol the rate of exchange had reached "export point"[1]. Since import necessarily implies export, it is obvious that when the rate of exchange between London and Bristol is at export point in Bristol it must be at import point in London.

We have thus seen that one cause of variations in the rate of exchange lies in changes in the relative indebtedness of the two countries. Another

[1] When the rate of exchange moves towards export point it is spoken of as an unfavourable exchange; when it moves towards import point it is termed a favourable exchange.

important cause lies in changes in the relative value of money, that is, in the rate of interest. Suppose, for instance, that owing to a trade revival in Bristol the demand for loans becomes keen, and the rate of interest rises to 6 per cent. ; while in London, where trade is stagnant, it remains at 2 per cent. It will, then, be profitable for a London capitalist to call in the money which he has lent out at 2 per cent., to buy with it a money order on Bristol, and to send the order to Bristol for encashment and investment at 6 per cent. Such an increased demand in London for money orders on Bristol, as we have already explained, will be met by an increase in the price of these orders, or, in other words, by a rise in the rate of exchange. If the trade revival in Bristol is but a small affair, it may be that the increased supply of credit in Bristol (causing a rise in prices) coupled with a withdrawal of credit in London (causing a fall in prices) will act in the manner already described, and will cause the relative appreciation in the Bristol rate of interest to disappear, and the rate of exchange to veer in the opposite direction without the necessity for shipping gold having arisen. But although there was no actual movement of gold there was, nevertheless, a tendency towards movement, and this tendency was shown by the variations in the rate of exchange. The rate of exchange is, in fact, a pointer showing the direction in which the gold

current tends to set, and the changes in this gold
current are the immediate causes of changes in the
rate of exchange. Changes in the rate of exchange
are sometimes spoken of as the causes of a contraction of credit or other similar movement; but
strictly speaking it is the change in the gold current,
of which the change in the rate of exchange is only
a sign, which is the true cause. A man may say that
he took out his umbrella because the barometer was
falling, but the real cause of his caution was the
presence of a cyclonic disturbance. Similarly the
bill-broker may say that he raised his rates because
the exchange was falling, but the real cause of his
action was the unfavourable set of the gold current.
It would, of course, be mere pedantry to object to
such statements as these, or to try to avoid the
slight fallacy which they involve by means of some
cumbrous circumlocution, but it is, nevertheless,
sometimes advantageous, when studying the complex
phenomena of the money market, to remember that
the rate of exchange is essentially an effect and not
a cause.

Up to this point we have supposed that both
London and Bristol have refrained from venturing
upon any unorthodox expedients, and have relied
upon gold as the sole medium for paying debts
whether at home or abroad. But now suppose that
the Bristol corporation, being in want of money,

decides to employ the device so well known to the South American Republics, the device of issuing paper money. It therefore prints a large number of pieces of paper, each with an elaborate device declaring that it is worth (say) £1, and enacts that every citizen of Bristol having a debt of £1 to pay shall be entitled to discharge himself by handing one of these notes to his creditor. The corporation, we will suppose, is £1,000,000 in debt, and it now discharges this debt by printing one million £1 notes and by using them to pay off its creditors. As a result of this payment it is obvious that one million £1 notes have been added to the circulation of the city, over and above all the gold that was in use before. But since there is no sudden increase of trade to require this great addition to the medium of exchange, the greater part of the new notes, or of the gold which they have displaced, will flow into the coffers of the banks, and will swell their cash balances ; for the notes, being good for all payments in Bristol, are practically as good as gold to the banks, and are therefore included in the term "cash." From this expansion of the supply of currency follow important consequences. The cash balances as we have already seen, are the basis upon which the bankers give loans, and an increase in the cash balances means, therefore, an increase of loans. But an increase of loans, again, means a rise of prices, and a rise of prices in Bristol means that people will leave off buying in Bristol and will begin to buy in London instead. The citizens of Bristol, in order to pay for their increased purchases in London, will buy money orders at the Bristol post office, and will send them to their creditors to cash at the London post office. Thus the cash balance of the post office at Bristol will increase, and in London it will diminish, until finally it will be necessary for the post office to send gold from Bristol to London. The effect of this, as has already been explained, is to lower prices in Bristol, and raise them in London, and so the effect of the issue of paper money by the Bristol corporation may be altogether compensated by the movement of gold from Bristol to London. But if the corporation, pleased at having discovered such an easy way of paying its debts, continues to make issues of paper money, each fresh issue will be followed by an outflow of gold from Bristol to London until the money in use at Bristol comes to consist almost entirely of notes. As a consequence of this, the payments made to the post office in the purchase of money orders on London will be composed less and less of gold and more and more of notes. But it is gold which the post office wants, for the notes are of no use for export, as nobody in London would think of taking them in payment of debts. The Bristol post office cannot, however, insist on being paid for its money orders in gold, for the notes are legal tender in Bristol and are a sufficient discharge for any debt.   It will be impossible to continue the sale of money orders on London at all, unless some means is devised of putting the London branch in funds and so enabling it to pay these orders when presented.   It is necessary, therefore, to devise some way of filling the coffers of the London branch, other than that of sending gold. The obvious plan is for the Bristol branch to use some of its superabundant notes in buying large quantities of (say) coal in Bristol, and to send this to London where it could be sold and the proceeds paid into the depleted balances of the post office there.   Whether this was done directly by the post office officials themselves, or indirectly by agents, the incidental expenses of commission and insurance, freight, etc., would be considerably more than the expenses of sending an equivalent value in gold, and the Bristol branch will therefore have to charge more for money orders, the sale of which necessitates such expenses, than it did for money orders the sale of which merely involved the shipment of gold.   But, in addition to all this, the Bristol branch has also to recoup itself for the loss caused by buying coal in Bristol, where prices are high (owing to the issues of paper money), and selling in London, where coal is relatively cheap.   Suppose, for instance, that coal is selling for 22*s*. per ton in Bristol, and 20*s*. in London, and that the expenses of shipment amount to 1*s*. per ton. It follows that the Bristol post office, in order to realise 20*s*. in London, must be prepared to spend 23*s*. in Bristol. Therefore it cannot afford to sell a 20*s*. money order on London for less than 23*s*. That is to say, the rate of exchange which, while there was gold available for export, could not rise above the "export point" of £1 0*s*. 3*d*., has now risen to £1 3*s*. 0*d*. And this is by no means the limit. If the issues of paper money were to be continued the price of coal might rise to 40*s*. in Bristol as against 20*s*. in London, and in that case (supposing that coal was the most convenient article of export) the exchange would stand at £2 1*s*. When a country is suffering from an over-issue of paper money, its exchange will depend upon the price which its principal exports fetch in gold in foreign markets as compared with the price which they fetch in paper in the home market.

CHAPTER V

THE FOREIGN EXCHANGE AND THE HYDRAULIC MODEL

REMEMBERING that the phenomena which we have outlined in the last chapter, upon the hypothesis of two isolated towns using gold coins of the same kind, are to be found occurring in an exactly similar way in the case of two countries using gold coins of different kinds, we are now in a position to extend

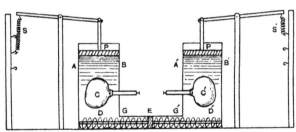

Fig. 2.

our hydraulic model so as to illustrate the subject of the foreign exchanges. For this purpose suppose that we have another cylinder $A'B'$[1] connected with

---

[1] See Fig. 2.

our former cylinder by a metal tube, and suppose that in this tube there is a closely fitting piston-head *E*, which slides along a wire passing through its centre. On either side of the piston-head springs are fixed in such a way that when no other forces are at work the piston-head will remain at its position of equilibrium mid-way between the two cylinders, and will tend to return to that position when displaced. That position represents the Mint par of exchange, and the movements of *E* represent the movements of the rate of exchange between the two countries represented by the two cylinders. The points *G* and *G'* represent the "gold points," for when the piston-head *E*, under pressure from the water in the cylinder *AB*, reaches *G'*, water flows freely into the cylinder *A'B'*. Similarly when *E* reaches *G* water flows freely from *A'B'* into *AB*, just as gold begins to flow when the exchange reaches gold point. The strength of the springs *D'* and *D* represents the expenses of shipping any given quantity of gold from *AB* to *A'B'*, and from *A'B'* to *AB* respectively. The two springs will probably be equal in strength, but it might be convenient, under certain circumstances, to consider one as being stronger than the other in order to represent hindrances placed in the way of the free export of gold, *e.g.* by the German Reichsbank.

Our second cylinder must be supposed fitted up

with credit bag, piston-head and the other appurtenances which we described in dealing with one cylinder
only. But it will be convenient, just for the moment, to
strip our model of all its complications, and to consider
two plain cylinders filled with water and connected
by a tube. If, now, we remember that the area of
the end of the cylinder represents the volume of
trade, that the water represents gold, and that the
height of the water represents prices, we have at
once a material illustration of two important truths.
Firstly, that where credit is undeveloped, the supply
of gold is shared between different countries in proportion to the volume of their trade. Secondly, that
when gold flows freely between two countries, the
level of prices in those countries tends to be the
same. The gold-standard countries of the world may
be considered as a set of such cylinders of various
and varying sizes, and all connected with each other
either directly or indirectly. Into some of these
cylinders (the gold-producing countries) water is
being continuously pumped in, and flows from them
to all the other cylinders. But, since even water
does not find its level immediately, the level of the
water will be higher in the former cylinders than in
the latter; that is, the general level of prices will be
higher in the gold-producing countries than in the
purely gold-consuming countries, and prices will be
lowest in those countries which have the least efficient

means of communication with the gold-producing countries.

Now, to return to the consideration of our two cylinders equipped with all the appurtenances already described, let us trace the changes which will take place in the whole system when any one of the parts is displaced from its position of equilibrium. First, suppose a sudden inflation of the credit bag C. As a consequence of this inflation the level of the water in the cylinder AB will rise, and the strain on the spring S will be relaxed. Owing to the rise in the level of the water the pressure on this side of the piston-head E will be greater than the pressure on the other side. The piston-head E will, therefore, move towards the cylinder $A'B'$. This movement will cause the water to rise in the cylinder $A'B'$, and will so relieve somewhat the differential pressure which is the cause of the movement itself. In addition to this there will be some slight resistance offered by the spring D'. But if the inflation of the bag C be great enough the piston-head E will be driven as far as G'. When it reaches this point there is free communication between the cylinders, water will rapidly flow through from AB until the level of the water is the same in both cylinders, and the piston head E, under the pressure of the spring D', will move back to its former central position. The final result of the change is that the credit-bag C is larger, the level of the water in both cylinders is higher, and there is less strain on the springs S and S'. Translating these changes from their mechanical into their money-market form we get the following series of events :—An inflation of credit in the country AB leads to a rise of prices and a fall of the rate of discount. This rise of prices, combined with a well-supplied money-market, favours an outward flow of gold and an unfavourable movement of the exchange. The inflation of credit, however, still continues until finally the exchange reaches export point and gold is sent in large quantities to the country $A'B'$. As a consequence of this the rate of discount in $A'B'$ falls and prices rise until the rate of exchange begins to return to its former level.

Another interesting series of changes occurs in consequence of a sudden collapse of the credit-bag. Suppose that the credit-bag C expands greatly. Then, as before, the level of the water in AB will rise, the strain on the spring S will be somewhat relaxed, and the piston-head E will move towards G'. If, now, the credit-bag C collapses there will be a great fall in the level of the water in AB, and a sudden increase of strain on the spring S; E will be forced violently back from the neighbourhood of G' until it reaches G, and water will begin to flow into the cylinder AB. That is to say, a sudden collapse of credit will produce a marked fall of prices and a great stringency in the money-market; the exchange will move rapidly to import point, and gold will flow into the country. Such a series of events was most dramatically illustrated by the American crisis of 1907.

We may now proceed to add further complications to our model in order to show the effects of the issue of inconvertible paper currency. For this purpose suppose that the tube shown as connecting the two cylinders is prolonged into the cylinder $A'B'$, and that the portion of the tube which lies within this cylinder is of a semi-permeable nature, so that it will allow water to pass through freely but will oppose an absolute barrier to the passage of gelatinous fluids. Suppose, then, that we take some gelatinous fluid (of the same specific gravity as water) and pump it into the cylinder AB by means of a pump (which is not shown on the diagram). This will cause the piston-head P to rise and the piston-head E to move towards G'. If more of the gelatinous fluid be pumped into AB these movements will continue until finally the piston-head E will reach G', and water will begin to flow through the semi-permeable membrane into the cylinder $A'B'$. Thus the differential pressure on E will be removed and the piston-head will move slowly back to its central position. This process we must imagine to be repeated again and again until finally all the water has been driven out of AB and the cylinder is full of the gelatinous fluid, which cannot escape into $A'B'$ owing to the semi-permeable membrane. When this state of affairs has been arrived at, it is obvious that by pumping in more and more of the fluid the piston-head E will be driven past G', and that, by continuing to pump, the piston-head P may be forced up to any desired height.

This forcing into the cylinder of a fluid which is unable to flow out again presents a very close analogy to the issue of paper money. Following out the movements which we have described as taking place on the model, we see that an issue of paper money is followed by a rise of prices, a fall in the rate of discount, and an unfavourable movement of the exchange. The issue of more paper will be followed by an outflow of gold which will temporarily relieve the pressure, and so cause a recovery of the exchange and a fall of prices. Repeated fresh issues of paper will cause more and more gold to be exported, until finally the time will come when there will be no more gold available for export. The export of gold, as we have seen, has two main results; it reduces the level of prices, and it prevents the exchange from falling below export point. If, then, the possibility of exporting gold be taken away, it follows that the exchange may become indefinitely unfavourable, and that the level of prices may rise to any height.

CHAPTER VI

THE BILL OF EXCHANGE

THE subject of the foreign exchanges deals in the main with the manufacture and sale of bills of exchange. But these invaluable instruments of modern commerce are of use not only to enable a debtor to pay a creditor living in a foreign country, but also to smooth over the difficulty arising from the fact that a seller usually wants immediate payment, whilst the buyer usually wants to defer payment until he has marketed the goods which he has bought. In order to evade this latter difficulty the bill of exchange is largely used in internal as well as in external trade. As an illustration of its use for this purpose let us suppose that A has sold corn to B to the value of £1,010. B says that he cannot pay for the corn until he has resold at any rate a portion of it; A, on the contrary, wishes to be paid at once. He therefore draws on B a bill of exchange to the following effect,

£1,010   London,
                                    September 28, 1909.

Three months after date pay to *A* or order the
sum of one thousand and ten pounds, for value
received.

    To *B*.   (Signed) *A*.

and sends the document to *B*. *B* on receiving it
writes across the face "accepted" (signed) "*B*";
thereby signifying that he is willing to comply with
A's order to pay £1,010 three months ahead, and
then returns the document to *A*. *A*, if he does not
wish to wait for three months and then get the full
face value from *B*, may take the bill to his banker *C*,
and sell the bill to him for a less sum "down." In
such case he is said to "discount" the bill[1]. If the
sum which *A*'s banker pays for the bill is £1,000, and
if at the end of the three months he presents the bill
to *B*, and recovers from him £1,010, the essence of
the transaction obviously is that the banker has
charged £10 (1) for a loan to *A* of £1,000 for three
months, (2) for the risk of not being able to recover

---

[1] *A* is known as the *drawer* of the bill, *B* is known as the *drawee*;
but after " accepting " the bill he is known as the *acceptor*. If *A*
discounts the bill with *C*, *C* becomes the *holder* of the bill. If *C*
signs his name on the back of the bill, and transfers the bill to *D*, *D*
becomes the holder, and *C* becomes an *indorser*, and is liable to pay
D if *B* fails to do so.

the money from *B*, and (3) for certain other risks
which we shall explain later. This rate of £10 for
£1,000 for three months, or rather its equivalent of
4 per cent. per annum, is said to be the rate of
discount paid by *A*. It is obvious that this rate
must depend largely on the demand for such loans
and the supply of money to satisfy them. If many
people want to borrow money by discounting bills,
the rate of discount will go up; if money is abundant,
it will go down. But the rate must also depend on
the financial position of *B*. If *B* is a man of straw
and likely to become a bankrupt at any moment, the
banker must charge very highly against the risk of
not being able to recover on the bill when the time
of payment arrives. In its normal, or perhaps it
would be more correct to say, in its original form,
the bill of exchange is drawn against merchandise of
some sort or another which has been sold to the
acceptor. But in many cases the negotiation of a
bill is merely a device for obtaining a loan. Thus if
A wishes to borrow from his banker he may draw a
bill on *B* as if in the course of a genuine transaction
of sale, and bring it to his banker for discount,
subsequently arranging with *B* as to how payment
shall be made when the bill matures. Such "accommodation bills" or "finance bills" are outwardly just
the same as bills which are based on an actual sale.
The wording of a "produce bill" is exactly the same

as the wording of a finance bill and each contains references to value received. The only difference is that in the one case the consideration is genuine, in the other it is fictitious ; but this difference does not appear upon the face of the bill, and it is therefore very difficult to know to which class any particular bill belongs. When, therefore, the banker is asked to discount a bill, it is not so much the nature of the bill to which he attends as the financial position of the drawer or acceptor. If the person who has undertaken the responsibility of paying the bill of exchange, that is the acceptor, is a man of well-known probity and ample resources, the banker will be willing to make a very small charge, or even no charge at all, for the risk of being met by a refusal to pay when the bill falls due. It has become the custom, therefore, for persons who wish to discount bills to pay a small commission in order to induce some firm of very high reputation to accept the bill, and so to enable them to discount it at a lower rate. Or the same effect may be obtained by paying some such firm to "indorse" the bill after it has been already accepted. The effect of the indorsement is that in the event of the acceptor failing to pay when the bill falls due, the indorsing firm will have to pay instead. The firms who thus trade upon their good name by accepting and indorsing bills are known as "accepting houses." They are the outposts of our system of credit, for it is, to a great extent, the accepting houses which have to decide to whom and how far credit is to be given. Within reasonable limits a banker will discount any bill accepted by a reputable accepting house, and therefore in the case of loans attempted to be raised by means of discounting bills, it is in effect the accepting house and not the banker who decides whether the loan shall be granted or not. If the accepting houses are too prodigal with their signatures the banks may easily be led into giving more loans than they are strictly justified in doing[1]. This power in the accepting house to make effective a demand for loans which otherwise might be ineffectual will require notice in connection with the subject of the foreign exchanges. Besides the accepting house and the banker, there are two other institutions which must be mentioned in dealing with bills of exchange. These are the bill broker and the discount house. The bill broker, speaking generally, is a firm or an individual who buys, or, in other words, discounts bills, not in order to hold them until they mature, as do the bankers, but in order to resell them at a profit. The dis-

[1] It is said that the London banks are gradually absorbing the business of acceptance themselves. If the banks conduct this business with as much prudence as the accepting houses, the change is a desirable one, for thus the machinery of credit will become more coherent and better organised. See Withers, *The Meaning of Money*, p. 163.

counting of bills is a business which requires an
enormous amount of special knowledge regarding the
financial status of drawers and acceptors ; and this
knowledge, to be of any use, must always be kept up
to date.   The bankers, therefore, may prefer to leave
all these special investigations to the bill broker, and
to buy bills out of the bill broker's stock.   The bill
broker always keeps a selection of bills in stock, and
so, by going to him, the banks are able to get just
that kind of bill which they require, in addition to
obtaining the advantage of his special knowledge.
In order to provide a good choice for his customers,
the bill broker must always have a number of bills
unsold, and this requires a certain amount of capital.
This capital the bill broker as a rule gets from the
banks in the form of loans from day to day or for
periods not usually exceeding a week.   The rate at
which such loans are given by bankers to bill brokers
or to discount houses is technically spoken of as the
" rate for money."

The " discount houses " are firms which have
passed beyond the stage of buying bills merely in
order to rediscount them with a banker.   Such firms,
indeed, are not above selling bills to a bank, but a
considerable portion of their stock they have bought
as investments, and intend to keep until the bills
mature.   The business of a discount house, it is
obvious, must require a considerable amount of

capital; much more than that of the bill broker, for instance, for the bill broker only keeps a small stock of bills in hand. The discount house obtains its capital not only, like the bill broker, by borrowing from the banks, but also by offering a small percentage to any person who will deposit money with them. But though in this way they manage to acquire large sums on deposit they do, nevertheless, rely upon the banks to supply a considerable proportion of their capital requirements.

We have now followed the bill of exchange through the earlier stages of its history. We have seen how the man who wants payment for goods which he has sold, or the man who has not sold goods but would like payment all the same, may attain his object through the medium of a bill of exchange; how the signature of some great accepting house converts this bill into a valuable security on which money may be borrowed; and how the holder of the bill may sell it to a discount house, or to a bill broker who will resell it to a banker. It remains to consider the position of the bill of exchange when it has reached a place of rest in the banker's portfolio.

CHAPTER VII

A BANKING BALANCE-SHEET

In a previous chapter we set out a banking balance-sheet in its most simplified form. But this form, though useful for the purposes of theoretical illustration, is too abstract to be applied to the actual facts of the money market, and we will therefore give a place to more technical distinctions and expand the balance-sheet as follows :—

Liabilities	£	Assets	£
Deposits of customers	20,000,000	Cash in hand and at Bank of England	4,000,000
		Loans at call and at short notice ...	2,000,000
		Bills discounted and advances ...	12,000,000
		Investments ...	2,000,000
	£20,000,000		£20,000,000

Such a specimen as this will enable us to explain

the most essential features of the balance-sheet of a London bank. The "deposits of customers," as was explained in our first chapter, does not consist only, as is often supposed, of savings temporarily intrusted to the bank by its customers. Some portion of this item, no doubt, does represent savings, but the larger part represents sums which have been lent by the bank to its customers in the form of book credits.

Next, turning to the "assets" side, we find the item "Cash in hand and at Bank of England." "Cash in hand" stands for the till-money which every banker keeps by him for the ordinary business of the day and that portion of his surplus gold which the banker chooses to put in his own hands. "Cash at the Bank of England" represents money which is not needed for the ordinary business of the day and also a reserve of cash for the time of crisis when there may arise a run upon the bank. "Cash in hand and at Bank of England" as a whole may be described as the banker's "first line of defence," for if there is any run upon the bank the banker will naturally satisfy the first applicants for payment by means of his till money and by drawing out his balance from the Bank of England. His second line of defence consists of "Loans at call and at short notice"; that is, money lent by the bank to bill-brokers and discount houses, both of these institutions, as we have already explained, being dependent upon loans from the banks in order to provide themselves with working capital. These loans they obtain at a very cheap rate, partly because they offer excellent security, and partly because they agree to repay the money lent either immediately they are asked to do so (in which case the loan is said to be at call) or else a few days after having been given warning (in which case the loan is said to be at short notice). To the banker the great point about these loans is that the money lent can be got in immediately or, at worst, after a few days, and so is available to meet sudden demands. But owing to the low rate of interest obtainable on such loans, he cannot afford to use more than a certain proportion of his money in this way, and is compelled, by motives of self-interest, to search out methods for its more remunerative employment. These methods are represented by the next item in our balance-sheet, viz. "Bills discounted and advances." It is obvious that good bills of exchange form almost ideal investments for a banker, for they generally afford excellent security and, when the date for payment arrives, realise themselves without any possibility of depreciation. There are, in fact, only two points of uncertainty. It may happen, as already suggested, that all the parties to the bill will be unable to meet their obligations. It may happen, also, that a pressing demand for cash will arise which will compel the banker, after exhausting the resource of calling in loans, to sell the bill at a loss[1]. But if one at least of the parties to the bill remains solvent and if the banker can afford to wait until the bill matures, there is no possibility of loss through depreciation as there is in the case of stocks and shares.

Last of all upon the "assets" side of our balance-sheet comes the item "Investments," denoting that the banker has put some of his money into stocks and shares. Since the returns obtained by investing money, even in the soundest of securities, such as Consols, compare favourably with the returns to be got by discounting bills, and are, moreover, obtainable without any of the worry involved in the choosing and constant renewing of suitable bills, it may seem surprising that the banker does not give up discounting altogether and put the money into gilt-edged securities instead. The explanation of the large sums which the banker, in fact, keeps invested in bills, lies in his desire for so-called liquid assets. Some portion of the stock of bills which he holds will probably mature every day, and so turn itself into money which the banker may either keep as money or re-invest in bills. Consols, on the other hand, do not become periodically

---

[1] This is the second of the two risks referred to in our last chapter, against which the banker must insure himself by an increased rate of discount, i.e. by lowering the price which he gives for the bill.

redeemable at par. If the banker is obliged to sell
Consols in order to satisfy some passing need for
ready money, he may have to sell at a loss, and he
certainly will have to pay a commission to his broker.
He prefers, therefore, to keep a large stock of bills,
which enables him to meet temporary fluctuations in
the demand for cash in a convenient and inexpensive
way. Hence it is that "investments" do not form
a larger proportion of the banker's assets.

Looking at the balance-sheet as a whole the most
important point for notice is the proportion of
"deposits of customers" to "cash in hand and at
the Bank of England." The former item represents
the largest amount which the bank could possibly
be required to pay to its customers; the latter represents the amount immediately available to meet such
a requirement; and the proportion between them
represents the strength of the bank's position. It
is, therefore, important for the banker to be able
to show a fair proportion of cash to liabilities when
he brings his balance-sheet before the public; and it
is generally supposed that in order to be able to do
this he calls in some of his loans just before the
arrival of the date of publication. By calling in
loans he diminishes "deposits of customers," or increases "cash," or both, and so gives to his statement
an appearance of praiseworthy prudence and modera-
tion. This allegation is supported by two facts; first,

that at the end of every month[1] and of every half year there is a relative difficulty in obtaining loans; second, that the banks do not refute their critics, as they might easily do, by publishing their average position throughout the month, instead of their position on one day only.

Up to this point we have treated of the relations of banks to their customers. We must now consider the relations of these banks amongst themselves. If at the end of any one day, as the result of transactions between their customers, there were due £1000 from Parr's bank to Lloyd's, £1000 from Lloyd's to Barclay & Co., and £1000 from Barclay & Co. to Parr's, and if there were no concerted action between the three banks, such a state of affairs would involve the sending of three messengers, each carrying £1000 in notes or gold, between one bank and another. But if, in pursuance of a mutual agreement, representatives of the three banks were to meet and cancel the liabilities of their respective banks one against the other, it would be found, under the circumstances described, that no payments at all were necessary, and much trouble and expense would be saved. Such an arrangement has in fact been made, and all the principal London banks belong to a "clearing house" to which all cheques received by them are

---

[1] A number of the principal London banks publish monthly balance sheets.

sent daily. Also, each "clearing" banker and the clearing-house itself has an account at the Bank of England. By this means it is possible to settle their mutual liabilities simply by means of transfers in the books of the Bank of England. By means of this system the banks are relieved of the expense of keeping an idle balance of notes to meet the "charges" of other banks, and also of the trouble of constantly sending notes or gold to those banks to which they are in debt. Of course the clearing bankers are not entirely relieved of all necessity to keep a balance for the requirements of a settlement amongst themselves. They do keep a balance, as stated above, at the bank of England for this and other purposes, and this balance is alleged to amount to a minimum of twenty million sterling.

As a result of our examination of a typical banking balance-sheet we see that bankers occupy a unique position in the commercial system, for they provide the credit which is a raw material for every industry. By their loans to bill-brokers and to discount-houses they determine the "rate for money," and so indirectly the rate of discount. They also affect the rate of discount directly by discounting bills themselves; and it is probable that they will pursue this branch of their business to a far greater extent in the future. By their loans to members of the Stock Exchange, again, the banker can affect the course of speculation and the price of stocks and shares. But all these activities pale before the importance of the banker's greatest function, the economising of gold, whereby industry has been released from its fetters of metal and allowed to expand freely within the almost boundless limits of an elastic system of credit.

CHAPTER VIII

THE FOREIGN EXCHANGES IN PRACTICE

In this chapter we purpose to treat of the nature of the exchange between a gold-using country and (1) another gold-using country, (2) a silver-using country, (3) a country with an inconvertible paper currency, and (4) a country which maintains a "gold exchange standard."

Firstly, then, as to the exchange between two gold-using countries, that is, between two countries having gold as their standard of value and medium of exchange. As an example of this case we may take the exchange between England and France. The foreign bill of exchange is the means whereby one nation discharges its indebtedness to another. When *A*, resident in London, wishes to pay a debt due to *B*, also resident in London, he sends to *B* a cheque, that is to say, an order to a London banker to pay a certain sum to *B*. When *A*, resident in London, wishes to pay a debt due to *C*, resident in Paris, he sends to *C* a bill on Paris, that is to say, an order to some person resident in Paris to pay a certain sum to C. In order to do this A will be obliged to have recourse to some person who has bills on Paris for sale. The great market for foreign bills is the Royal Exchange, where the exchange brokers meet every week on Tuesdays and Thursdays. It is the interaction of supply and demand in this market which determines the rate at which A will be able to buy his bill ; and supply and demand, again, are determined by certain causes which we shall now attempt to analyse. Since the majority of bills are drawn against consignments of merchandise, the supply of bills on France must depend largely upon the value of the goods lately sold by England to France ; but to this amount must be added the bills drawn against "invisible exports" of services, for which France is indebted to England under the head of freight, insurance and all manner of charges by way of commission. On the other hand, the demand for bills on France is chiefly due to those who have debts to pay in France, and will therefore depend largely upon the value of the merchandise lately sold by France to England. If, then, the state of trade between the two countries is such that England owes just as much to France as France does to England, the demand for, and supply of, bills on France will be exactly equal, and the exchange will be at par, *i.e.* about 25·22 francs. Such a state of things can seldom occur, and it will generally happen that the balance of trade is in favour of one country or another. Suppose that the balance of trade is in favour of France, *i.e.* that England has lately been buying more from France than France has been buying from England. In such case many English merchants will have debts to pay in France and the demand for bills on France will be keen. On the other hand, since the consignments of goods to France have been comparatively small, fewer bills have been drawn and the supply of bills on France will be restricted. Hence, when the supply of trade bills has been bought up there will still be a demand for more, and this demand may be satisfied through the agency of the "foreign banker." The foreign banker is one who has agents in the principal monetary centres, and who will draw bills on these agents and sell the bills to any person who requires them. When he sells such bills the foreign banker imposes upon his agents the liability of meeting the bills, and he is therefore obliged to make arrangements for re-imbursing to his agents the amount which they have paid out to the holders of the bills. How is he to do this? A shipment of gold is the obvious solution, but this is an expensive transaction, and in practice it is usual to buy up bills on those countries whose exchanges provide the best terms, and to remit these bills as cover for the liability of the agents. The foreign banker referred to might, for instance, buy bills on Germany and send these bills to Paris. The Paris branch could then sell the bills on Germany and thus obtain sufficient funds to meet the bills drawn against it by the London branch. It might be, however, that the demand of the foreign banker for bills on Germany and other countries (other than France) would so raise their price or, in other words, would so turn the exchanges of these countries against England[1] that it would be just as cheap to ship gold as to send bills. There is, nevertheless, another resource of which the bill-merchant may take advantage before he is compelled to resort to the shipment of gold. This resource is found in the so-called "international" securities, such as bonds of the Italian, Egyptian, Russian and other governments which have a ready sale upon all the bourses of Europe. The bill-merchant who has exhausted the possibilities of bills can fall back upon the expedient of buying blocks of these securities and sending them to the agent or branch which is in need of money. The agent can then sell the securities

[1] It should be noted that when the balance of indebtedness between country A and country B is in favour of B, and the bill merchants of A fill up the gap by buying bills on country C, and by sending them to B, the effect of this is (1) as between A and C, to turn the exchange in favour of C, (2) as between B and C to turn the exchange in favour of B. Or, speaking more generally, all the other exchanges will tend to become unfavourable to A and favourable to B.

and so place himself in funds. Finally, it may happen
that the increased purchases of these securities in
England, and their increased sales in France, causes
their price to rise in England and to fall in France
to such an extent that the bill-merchant will be
driven to his last expedient, *i.e.* the shipment of
gold. These transactions, whether the purchases and
sales of bills and securities or the shipment of gold,
all involve expense, and the person who applies to
the foreign banker for the bills which necessitate
such expenses must pay for the expenses as well
as for the face value of the bill at the mint par of
exchange. So long as bills on other countries are
available at a reasonable price these expenses will
be small, and the price of a bill on France will be
only slightly above its face value at the mint par
of exchange; when bills are exhausted, and the
foreign banker has recourse to securities, expenses
will rise somewhat, and with them the price of bills
on France. Finally, when gold has to be shipped,
incidental expenses will be at their maximum, exchange will be at export point and the price of bills
at the corresponding level. Having studied the
effects of the relative indebtedness of two countries
upon their exchanges, we must now describe the
effects of differences in the value of money. But
before starting upon this new topic, it will be necessary to advert more particularly to the subject of

the "long bill," *i.e.* a bill which is payable in several months' time, as opposed to the "short bill" or "cheque"[1] which is payable immediately. If A, a debtor living in London, wishes to pay his creditor B, living in Paris, by means of a bill of exchange, he has two alternatives. He may either pay B by means of a cheque, or he may pay by means of a bill payable in (say) three months' time. If A pays by cheque, B will be able to cash the cheque immediately it arrives. If A pays by means of a ninety days' bill, B will have to wait for his money for three months after the bill has reached him. Obviously, then, the face value of the ninety days' bill must be larger than the face value of the cheque. But the question, How much larger? is one which requires detailed discussion. To begin with, we have the equation:—

Value of cheque to B = Value of ninety days' bill to B,

since either might be sent to B in payment of the same debt. If B is paid by bill he will not only have to wait for his money (unless he discounts the bill), but he will also have to bear the risk of both the drawer and the acceptor failing before the date of payment arrives. Our equation, therefore, may be expanded as follows:—

---

[1] In its strict legal sense a cheque is a bill of exchange drawn upon a banker and payable on demand. But commercially a cheque is a bill payable on demand, no matter on whom it may be drawn.

Value of cheque to B = Face value of bill — interest
    for three months at the Paris rate of discount
    — risk estimated in money.

From our equation we see, then, that the price of
a long bill depends upon the sight rate, upon the
rate of discount prevailing in the country where the
bill is payable, and upon the state of credit.

Having thus glanced at the problem of the long
bill and its price, we must return to our discussion of
the effect which the value of money has upon the
sight rate. This effect is produced through the action
of those who invest their money in long bills on
different countries, and choose the bills of those
countries which give the best return. The bills
which give the best return are obviously those drawn
upon the country where the rate of discount is
highest; for the rate of discount is simply a measure
of this return. If the discount rate is higher in
Berlin than in London, the London banker will
prefer to invest in German rather than in English
bills. But the purchase of long bills on Germany
must be reckoned for in the balance of trade just
as must the purchase of German three per cents. or
of any other German securities. The relative supe-
riority of the Berlin rate of discount, by inducing
capitalists in London to buy German long bills, will
thus turn the balance of trade in favour of Germany,
and the favourable balance of trade, as has already

been explained, will cause an increased demand in England for short bills on Germany and so raise their price. Thus a rise in the Berlin bank-rate will tend to make the foreign exchanges favourable to Germany.

Of course such a means of influencing the exchanges can only be a temporary expedient; just as when a man who owes money to another induces him to extend the time of re-payment by offering to pay a higher rate of interest. The present stringency may be relieved, but increased liabilities have been incurred for the future. If, when the bills which England has bought fall due for payment, the balance of indebtedness is still against Germany, this deficit must be met by the shipment of gold unless the Berlin rate of discount can be raised to a point which will induce England not only to renew the bills which are maturing but also to buy others as well. If, on the other hand, when the bills mature, Germany's adverse balance of trade has disappeared, and the Berlin rate of discount is, nevertheless, maintained at its relatively high level, it may be profitable for England to continue buying such bills. But since England has no balance of indebtedness in its favour it will have to buy the bills, if it wishes to buy at all, by shipping gold. We see, then, that the attractiveness of long bills on any country as investments can be changed by changing the rate of discount in that country, and the power of so acting upon the exchanges may be utilised for two purposes.   First, to make up for any merely temporary unfavourable balance of trade, and so to obviate the necessity for a constant ebb and flow of gold.   Second, to attract gold to a country where it is required, owing to a sudden panic or some other cause quite apart from any consideration of the balance of trade.

2. THE SILVER EXCHANGES.

The case of the exchange between a country where the legal tender is gold and a country where there is a free coinage of legal tender silver, has now lost much of its importance.   Until recent years India, Japan and China were numbered amongst the "silver" countries, but since the closing of the Indian mints to silver in 1893 and the adoption of a gold standard by Japan in 1897, China remains the only important example of a silver-standard country.   But since the exchange between England and India has long been a classical example with economists, we propose to illustrate this class of cases with reference to the Indian exchange before 1893.

The first point which we have to observe is, that between a gold-standard country and a silver-standard country there cannot be any mint par of exchange. The mint par of exchange, as already explained, is

simply the physical relation which subsists between
different weights of the same substance, and which
cannot change unless those weights are changed.
There can be no such par between different weights
of different substances. But there can be, if we may
so term it, a "market par of exchange" which will
change from day to day and from hour to hour.
Thus if one country has a gold coin weighing an
ounce, and the other country a silver coin of similar
weight, and if, at any given moment, the market
price of an ounce of gold is thirty-five times the
market price of an ounce of silver, then, at that
moment, the market par of exchange will be thirty-
five, *i.e.* thirty-five silver coins will be equivalent
to one gold coin. Corresponding to this figure there
will be export and import points, showing the limits
within which the exchange must be confined so long
as the price of an ounce of gold remains thirty-five
times as much as the price of an ounce of silver. We
see, therefore, that a gold and silver exchange depends
primarily upon the ratio between the values of gold
and silver, and only to a very minor degree upon the
relative indebtedness of the two countries and the
value of money in their markets. In the case of
the exchange between England and India before
1893, the market par of exchange was $\frac{1}{240} \cdot \frac{2}{3}(X+1)$;
X being the price of silver in pence per ounce. That
is, 1 rupee was equivalent to $\frac{1}{240} \cdot \frac{2}{3}(X+1)$ pounds

stirling, or to $\frac{2}{3}(X + 1)$ pence. Accordingly, when
the price of silver fell from 60d. per ounce in 1872 to
39d. in 1891 there was a progressive fall in the Indian
exchange from 23d. to 15d. The consequences of
this fall were of such importance, that it may be
advisable to refer very shortly to the much-discussed
question of Indian currency. For the benefit of those
readers who are unacquainted with the outlines of
Indian finance, it is necessary to explain that the
Government of India, while drawing all its revenues
in silver in India, is obliged to make heavy payments
in gold in England. To meet these "home charges"
the Secretary of State for India sells "Council bills,"
that is, bills on India payable in silver in India. An
English merchant who owes (say) Rs 10,000 in India
will buy Council bills to that amount and remit
them to his creditor, who will then be able to draw
Rs 10,000 from some Government treasury in India.
It is obvious, then, that the sale of Council bills is
equivalent to the sale of so many rupees, and that
a fall in the gold value of the rupee means that more
rupees will have to be sold in order to meet a given
amount of home charges. Thus, if the home charges
are £10,000, and the rupee is worth 2s., the Secretary
of State will have to sell Council bills to the amount
of Rs 100,000. If the rupee falls to 1s. the sale of
bills would have to be increased to Rs 200,000 ; that
is, the actual payments made out of Indian revenues

would have been doubled, though the home charges themselves had not increased.

Harassed by the ever-increasing burden of home charges the Indian Government as early as 1878 proposed the introduction of a gold standard, but it was not till 1893 that this proposal finally received the sanction of the home Government. In June of that year, according to the recommendations of Lord Herschell's committee, the Indian mints were closed to silver. It was further announced that rupees would be given in exchange for gold delivered at the mints, and that Government dues might be paid in gold, the rate in each case being fifteen rupees for one sovereign. In spite of these measures the rupee continued to fall in value until January, 1895, when it reached the minimum of $12\frac{1}{2}d$. After that date, however, there was a steady rise, and from the end of 1897 the rupee remained steadily at or about $16d$. Practically speaking, India now had a gold standard, and in 1898 a committee was appointed to consider what further measures should be taken. As a result of their recommendations[1], the Indian mints were opened to the free coinage of gold, and both the rupee and the sovereign were declared to be legal tender at a ratio of fifteen to one. It must be noted, however, that no undertaking was given by the Indian Government to give gold in exchange for

[1] *Report of Indian Currency Committee*, 1899, (C. 9390).

rupees. The result of these two measures has been
satisfactory, and, with the exception of a few days
in 1907, the exchange has kept above its lower gold
point. The sovereign, however, in spite of its quality
of legal tender, has not been adopted to any extent
as part of the circulation, of the country. Hence,
when gold is required for export it cannot be taken
out of circulation neither can it be demanded *as of
right* from the Government in exchange for rupees.
India, therefore, strictly speaking, does not possess
a gold standard. Its standard has been described
as a "gold exchange standard," and will be referred
to in detail in a subsequent section.

3. THE "GOLD-PAPER" EXCHANGE.

We have seen that the Indian Government, by
closing its mints to the coinage of silver, was able to
give a scarcity value to those rupees which remained
in circulation; so that the value of the rupee as a
coin became greater than its value as a piece of
silver. By this device of restriction a scarcity value
can be given to any medium of exchange. Thus,
if the English Government were to declare that
Bank of England notes were to continue to be legal
tender, but that no gold should be given in exchange
for them, then, if the issues were kept within bounds,

they might still continue to circulate at their full
face value.   But supposing that for any reason, such
as a contraction of trade, the amount of bank notes
in circulation were to become relatively excessive
for the needs of the country, then these bank notes
would become depreciated, and would exchange for
a less weight of gold than they did before.   An
excellent historical example of such a state of affairs
may be found in the English "Bank restriction" of
1797—1819.   In February, 1797, there arose a sudden
panic caused by the arrival of a French frigate in
one of the Welsh harbours, and the public hastened
to withdraw their balances from the hands of the
country bankers.   The Newcastle banks were compelled to stop payment, and the coffers of the Bank
of England were seriously depleted.   Even at the
beginning of the crisis the stock of gold held by the
Bank of England was very small, and it soon became
apparent that this stock was not sufficient to satisfy
the demands of the public and of the bankers.   The
Bank of England was therefore obliged to apply to
Parliament for assistance, and their application was
met by the passing of an Act which provided that :
(1) the Bank should cease to pay its creditors in cash,
(2) payments of debts in bank notes should be deemed
payment in cash, if offered and accepted as such,
(3) bank notes should be received at par in payment
of taxes.   For some time after the passing of the

Act, the notes of the Bank of England, being restricted in amount, continued to exchange for the
same weight of gold as before, and the foreign
exchanges remained favourable.   But after a few
years the directors of the Bank, being relieved from
the necessity of maintaining an adequate reserve of
gold to insure the convertibility of their notes, and
thus being deprived of all incentive to restrict their
issues, began to make loans upon a large scale.   The
effect of this policy was soon seen.   The market
price of gold (as measured in notes) rose, in 1810,
to £4. 10s. 0d. (the mint price being £3. 17s. 10½d.),
thus showing that the notes had depreciated by 15½
per cent.   The foreign exchanges, also, became very
unfavourable, the exchange with Paris being 14 per
cent. below par.   Accordingly, a committee, known
to history as the "Bullion Committee," was appointed
to inquire into the causes of, and remedies for, this
unfortunate condition of affairs.   In giving evidence
before this committee the directors of the Bank of
England stated that, in their opinion, the high market
price of gold was due, not to the depreciation of
notes, but to the appreciation of gold, and that the
unfavourable state of the exchanges was due to an
adverse balance of indebtedness.   They stated, moreover, that there could be no possible excess in the
issue of Bank of England paper so long as the advances in which it was issued were made upon the

principle which then guided the conduct of the
directors, that is, so long as the discounts of mer-
cantile bills were confined to paper of undoubted
solidity arising out of real commercial transactions,
and payable at short and fixed periods. The committee, however, in their report exposed the fallacy
of these opinions, and showed (1) that the rise in the
market value of gold must be attributed to the
depreciation of the notes, since the price of gold as
measured in gold coin of the same fineness could
obviously not alter except by a very small quantity ;
(2) that since the expenses of sending gold to France
did not exceed about 7 per cent., no greater depression of the exchange than 7 per cent. could be
attributed to an unfavourable balance of trade, and
that the residual depression must be caused by a
depreciation of the currency; (3) that the principle
laid down by the directors for regulating their issues
was entirely unsound, and that the only safe guide
was the state of the exchanges and the price of gold
bullion. The only remedy for all these evils was the
resumption of cash payments, and, accordingly, the
committee recommended that cash payments should
be resumed within two years. The House of Commons,
however, far from confirming the recommendations
of the Report, passed a resolution controverting the
principles upon which these recommendations were
based, and thus encouraged the directors of the Bank

of England to persevere in the course which had already proved so disastrous. In consequence of further issues of paper the market price of gold continued to rise until, in 1813, it reached its maximum height of £5. 10s. 0d. During this year, however, there arose a great speculative mania which was followed in due course by a heavy tale of failures extending over several years. Amongst these failures were eighty-nine country banks, and the issues of country paper were enormously reduced. This violent reduction in the quantity of the circulating medium caused a general improvement in the monetary situation, and whereas, in May, 1815, the paper price of gold was £5. 6s. 0d., and the exchange on Paris 19, in October, 1816, the paper price of gold was £3. 18s. 6d., and exchange on Paris 26.10. This improvement, however, was not maintained, and in 1818 the Continental exchanges again began to set against England, and gold flowed rapidly out of the country. The directors of the Bank of England still refused to safeguard their reserve of gold by calling in loans, and it soon became evident that if they persisted in this course of conduct serious difficulties would arise. Committees of both Houses were appointed in 1819 to consider this question, and the result of their inquiry was a triumphant vindication of the principles laid down by the Bullion Committee in 1810. Accordingly, by a Statute of 1819, it was enacted that cash payments should be gradually resumed, the process to be finally completed by May 1st, 1823. Also the trade in gold bullion and coin was declared free from all restraints.

From a consideration of the English Bank restriction it is obvious that in the case of a "gold-paper" exchange there can be neither a mint par nor a market par of exchange. The rate of exchange, as has been explained in a previous chapter, depends almost entirely upon the relation between the level of prices in the gold-using country and the level of prices in the paper-using country. The level of prices in the paper-using country is determined by the proportion which the quantity of paper bears to the volume of trade. If trade expands, prices will fall, the value of the paper currency will rise, and the exchanges will become more favourable. If fresh issues of paper are made without a concomitant increase of the volume of trade, prices will rise, the value of the paper will fall, and the exchanges will move unfavourably. Changes in the rate of exchange due to the balance of indebtedness and the value of money cannot be isolated.

We have thus seen that in the case of a country with an inconvertible paper currency the foreign exchanges cannot be left to themselves, as in the case of a gold-standard country. The issue of paper must be regulated with direct reference to the exchanges. An expansion of this principle forms the subject of the next section.

4. THE GOLD EXCHANGE STANDARD.

In the last section we have seen that in order to maintain an inconvertible paper currency at its face value, or, in other words, to maintain the exchanges of that country at their proper level, the amount of paper in use must be regulated in accordance with the state of the exchanges. If the exchanges become adverse some of the paper currency must be withdrawn. If the exchanges become unduly favourable more paper must be issued. And the same principles apply to silver tokens.

Now suppose that the Government of a certain island had induced the inhabitants to use nothing but notes for all purposes of internal commerce, such notes being inconvertible and of the nominal values of one pound sterling and the fractions of a pound. How could such a Government regulate the issue of notes so that they would be really as well as nominally equivalent to the corresponding English coins? The value of (say) a one pound note may be prevented from rising above the value of a sovereign by enacting that the Government shall give one pound notes freely in exchange for gold at the rate of one note

for every sovereign or its equivalent weight of gold.
Then, if the value of the note were to rise unduly, it
would immediately be possible to make a profit by
importing gold and exchanging it for notes ; and in
practice this possibility would prevent the value of
the note from rising above its face value as measured
in gold. But to prevent the value of the note from
falling below its proper level is a more difficult
operation. Of course in countries such as England,
where there is a gold circulation, it is easy enough to
keep the paper currency at its face value by making
the notes redeemable in gold. The Government of a
gold exchange standard country cannot, and does not,
undertake to provide gold in that country, but it
does undertake to provide gold in other countries,
i.e. to sell bills on these countries. The sale of bills
on any country is obviously equivalent, in all its
effects, to the provision of gold for export to that
country, provided that the price of bills be adjusted
to allow for the fact that the buyer of the bill, if he
could not have got a bill, and had been obliged to
send gold, would have had to bear the expenses of
shipping this gold. So long as bills are freely sold at
that price it is obvious that the exchange cannot fall
below "export point," or rather below that point
which would have been export point had there been
gold available for export.

If we suppose that the people of our hypothetical

island trade with England, and that the price of sending a sovereign from one island to another is a penny, then the Government of this island, in order to establish a gold exchange standard, will have to undertake, (1) to give the local notes to any amount in exchange for their face value in gold, (2) to sell bills on London to any required amount at a rate not higher than £1 0s. 1d. (in local notes) for a bill on London for £1. In connection with this official or demi-official sale of bills we must draw attention to a point of importance, viz. that the currency received in exchange for bills sold must not be put back into general circulation. The reason for this precaution is as follows:—In the case of a country with a true gold standard, if the exchanges become unfavourable, the outward flow of gold restricts the currency, and so tends to raise the rate of discount and lower prices, thus bringing into action forces which tend to check the outflow of gold or even to reverse the current. In the case of a country with a gold exchange standard the sale of bills on foreign countries takes the place of an outflow of gold, and should therefore have the same effect of contracting the currency. This it will not do unless the token coins or paper received as the price of such bills are withdrawn altogether from active circulation, and kept so withdrawn until a demand for more currency is manifested by renewed offers of gold in exchange therefor.

We may illustrate these principles very briefly by reference to existing facts. The currency of India consists of rupees, which are token coins kept at a scarcity value by the closure of the mints to the free coinage of silver. The Indian Government gives rupees for gold at the rate of 15 rupees for £1. Out of the profits of coinage a "Gold Standard Reserve" has been built up. This reserve is held in London in the form of gilt-edged securities[1]. When required, bills on London are sold, and are met by the sale of securities from the reserve. The rupees received in payment for these bills are kept out of circulation.

The currency of the Philippines consists of silver pesos which circulate at a scarcity value. Out of the profits of coinage a reserve has been formed, and this is held in the form of deposits with New York bankers. New York drafts are sold by the Philippine Treasury, and the pesos received in payment are withdrawn from circulation.

The currency of Austria-Hungary consists of notes not redeemable in gold[2]. The Austro-Hungarian bank gives notes in exchange for gold at a fixed rate. The bank keeps a large stock of gold and of "devisen" (foreign bills). These bills are sold freely

[1] Since the crisis of 1907—08, a portion of the reserve has been held in the form of cash at short notice.

[2] A considerable quantity of legal tender silver gulden still exists, but it is gradually being withdrawn, and coined into small change.

when required, and at a rate not higher than the hypothetical export point, but the gold is not given for export. The bank itself, however, frequently exports gold in order to buy bills.

In addition to the countries already mentioned, Mexico and the Straits Settlements also maintain a gold exchange standard.

It is interesting to compare the gold exchange standard with the, so-called, "limping standard" (étalon boiteux), of which the French currency system offers a prominent example. In France the gold Napoleon is legal tender, but so is the silver five franc piece. The latter is a token coin kept at a scarcity value by restriction upon its coinage, just as is the rupee. Inasmuch as in India the gold sovereign is equally legal tender with the silver rupee, it might be said that India also possesses a limping standard : but the case of India, and, indeed, of all gold exchange standard countries, differs from the case of France in that (1) the Government of India keeps up in support of the exchange an elaborate mechanism which is not required in France, (2) in France there is a large circulation of gold, whereas, in India, the circulation of gold is very small. If the Bank of France, in the exercise of its legal powers, refuses to redeem its notes in gold, and insists upon paying for them with the legal tender five franc piece, it is possible, owing to the large use of gold for every day transactions, to collect and export gold. Such a device as this is not possible in countries where there is little or no gold in circulation. If the use of gold coins were to increase largely in India it might be possible for the Indian Government to abolish their gold standard reserve, in which case the gold exchange standard would become a " limping standard."

CHAPTER IX

THE BANK OF ENGLAND

IT is interesting to remember that the Bank of England, *the* bank par excellence of the modern world, was founded more than two hundred years ago ; in 1694, to be precise ; only thirty years after the time when Samuel Pepys chartered a hackney carriage in order to carry his accumulated guineas out into the country, and there bury them. That incident shows in the most vivid way what a revolution has been brought about by the development of banking. Imagine the effect upon industry if the well-to-do man of A.D. 1900 were to put his savings into his garden instead of into his bank! But the greater part of the history of the Bank of England, though full of interest, is not germane to our present purpose, and we therefore propose to limit this chapter to a short description of its modern development.

In a previous chapter[1] we have described the course of events during the period of the restriction, and have shown how the Bank Directors of the time

[1] Chapter VIII.

regulated their issues of notes solely with reference to the amount of real bills offered for discount; how the effect of this policy was to cause a depreciation of the notes, amounting at one time to 29 per cent., and how, in 1819, the Government, being at length converted to the principles set forth in the report of the Bullion Committee, ordered a resumption of specie payments. The next formal statement of the policy of the Bank Court with regard to the issue of notes may be found in the evidence given by the Governor of the Bank before a secret Committee of the House of Commons in 1832. According to his statement the ideal of the Bank was, (1) at a time when the exchanges were at par, to have two-thirds of their assets in the form of securities, and one-third in the form of bullion; (2) to keep the amount of securities as nearly as possible at the same level; the object of this plan being the attainment of a self-adjusting currency. Looking, for example, at a skeleton balance-sheet,

Liabilities		Assets	
Deposits	125	Securities	100
Notes outstanding	25	Bullion	50
	150		150

we see that if the "securities" are kept at 100 no notes can be issued except against an increase of "bullion." Also, if notes are brought to the

Bank, gold can be had in exchange. The weak point of the scheme, however, is that not only the possessors of notes but also the possessors of deposits can demand gold from the Bank. It might happen, for instance, that depositors would ask for gold to the amount of 40, in which case our skeleton balance-sheet would appear as follows :—

Liabilities		Assets	
Deposits	85	Securities	100
Notes outstanding	25	Bullion	10
	110		110

Such a drain of gold occurred in 1836 and again in 1839, and gave rise to the theory that the Bank was not keeping a sufficient reserve of gold to secure its issues. Accordingly Sir Robert Peel decided to remedy the defect of the scheme of 1832, and to prevent the depositors from trenching upon the gold required to support the note issue by separating the issue department of the Bank of England from its banking department. The principal provisions of the Bank Charter Act of 1844 were as follows :—

(1) The Bank of England to transfer to the new issue department securities to the amount of £14,000,000 (of which the debt due from the Government to the Bank was to be a part), and all the bullion and coin not required for the business of the banking department. The issue department to

deliver to the banking department notes to the value of the securities and bullion so transferred. No further issues of notes to be made from the issue department except in exchange for bullion. No bullion to be given out from the issue department except in exchange for notes. Every note, therefore, issued beyond the amount of £14,000,000 was to be backed by metal.

(2) Of the bullion kept in the issue department one-fifth might be silver[1].

(3) Any person to be entitled to demand notes from the issue department in exchange for standard gold bullion at the rate of £3 17s. 9d. per ounce.

(4) All existing banks of issue, other than the Bank of England, to be allowed to retain their privilege of issuing notes, to an amount equal to the average of their past issues during the early months of 1844.

(5) If any such bank should cease to issue notes, the Crown, in Council, to have power to authorise the Bank of England to extend its issues against securities by an amount not exceeding two-thirds of the amount of notes so withdrawn from circulation.

(6) Save the Bank of England and the existing banks of issue, no other bank to have power to issue notes.

[1] The object of this provision was that silver might be available for export to the silver-using countries of the Continent.

(7) Weekly accounts to be published.

Let us illustrate the working of the Act as shown by changes in our skeleton balance-sheet.   If, before the commencement of the Act, the balance-sheet was as follows :—

Liabilities		Assets	
Deposits	125	Securities	100
Notes outstanding	25	Gold ...	50
	150		150

after the commencement of the Act it would be as follows :—

Issue Department

Liabilities		Assets	
Notes issued	40	Securities	14
		Gold ...	26
	40		40

Banking Department

Deposits	125	Securities	86
		Gold ...	24
		Notes ...	15
	125		125

It has been assumed that the banking department needs 24 of gold for its business. This department has, therefore, handed over to the issue department the remaining 26 of gold together with 14 of securities, amounting to 40 in all.   In return the issue department has handed over notes to the amount of 15, which, together with the 25 in circulation, amounts to 40.

It was the intention of the framers of the Act of 1844 entirely to withdraw the regulation of the currency from the hands of the directors, but they would seem to have overlooked two important factors in the problem. First, that by extending their book credits, *i.e.* by increasing deposits, the directors could act upon the level of prices, and so upon the exchanges, just in the same way as by an increase in their issue of notes. Second, the depositors, by withdrawing their deposits in gold, could obtain gold for export without causing any contraction in the circulation of notes. Owing to the operation of these factors, the Bank Charter Act has failed in two of its main objects. Its objects, according to Sir Robert Peel, were (1) to prevent, by early and gradual contraction, the severe and sudden contractions of credit such as had occurred in 1836 and 1839, (2) to maintain the convertibility of the paper currency, (3) to prevent the fostering of undue speculation by an abuse of paper credit. The first hope was blighted by the crises of 1847, 1857 and 1866. The third rests upon the fallacy of supposing that prices are affected by an excess of the medium of circulation but not by an excess of book credits.

We may now turn to a detailed consideration of the weekly balance-sheet of the Bank of England in the form prescribed by the Act of 1844. A specimen of this return is reproduced below:—

An account pursuant to the Act 7 and 8 Vict. cap. 32, for the week ended on Wednesday, the 17th day of November, 1909.

Issue Department

Liabilities	£	Assets	£
Notes issued ...	52,500,395	Government debt	11,015,100
		Other securities	7,434,900
		Silver bullion ...	....
		Gold coin and bullion ...	34,050,395
	£52,500,395		£52,500,395

Banking Department

Proprietors' capital	14,553,000	Govt. securities	16,007,788
Rest	3,142,256	Other securities	22,906,803
Public deposits[1] ...	6,320,867	Notes	24,068,905
Other deposits ...	40,228,009	Gold and silver	
Seven day and other bills	34,128	coin	1,294,764
	£64,278,260		£64,278,260

[1] Including Exchequer, Savings banks, Commissioners of National Debt, and Dividend accounts.

Firstly, as to the return of the issue department, we have to notice that the amount of notes shown therein is not all held by the public. It is the practice of the banking department to hand over to the issue department all their spare gold, and to take

notes in exchange. The banking department, as may
be seen from the return, holds notes to the value of
£24,068,905, so that the value of the notes in circulation, and held by banks, is only £28,431,490. On
the assets side the first item is the Government debt
of eleven millions which, by the Act of 1844, was
specified as a portion of the fourteen millions' worth
of securities against which notes might be issued.
Next we find "other securities" to the value of
nearly seven-and-a-half millions, which, together with
the Government debt, amounts to eighteen-and-a-half
millions. The increase of the fiduciary issue by four-
and-a-half millions beyond the amount of fourteen
millions specified in the Act is accounted for by the
absorption of the issues of country banks. When all
existing separate issues have been absorbed, the
fiduciary issue of the Bank of England will amount
to nearly twenty millions. "Gold coin and bullion"
represents the non-fiduciary issue of the Bank. Every
note issued beyond the amount of the fiduciary issue
must be backed by gold, and is, literally speaking, as
good as gold. The power given to the directors of the
bank by the Act of 1844, to hold one-fifth of the metal
reserve of the note issue in silver, is not made use of.

With regard to the return of the Banking Department, the first item on the liability side is "pro-
prietors' capital," an item which needs no explanation.
Next comes the "rest." This is a reserve of undivided

profits which is never allowed to fall below the amount of £3,000,000. It is, therefore, possible, by observing the amount of the "rest" immediately before the half-yearly distribution of dividends, and by deducting £3,000,000 from that amount, to calculate how much will be available for distribution amongst the shareholders. The "public deposits" are nothing less than the current account of the British Government. Into this account all the taxes are ultimately paid, and from it all Government disbursements are made. Some taxes, such as excise receipts, come in fairly regularly during the whole year, but others, such as income tax and inhabited house duty, are collected mainly during the first quarter of the year. The rate of Government disbursements, on the other hand, is distributed fairly evenly over the whole year, but necessarily shows sudden increases on the dates when salaries are payable or dividends are due. Since the public income is abnormally large during the months of January, February and March, while expenditure is more evenly distributed, it follows that the "public deposits" must show a considerable increase in amount during the three months of increased receipts. This increase is, in fact, a well-known feature of the London money market. Indeed, nearly all the important changes in amount of this item occur at regular intervals, and can generally be predicted beforehand. "Public deposits," in the eyes of the banker, is an ideal account; for an account the changes in which can be foreseen months beforehand is almost as good as an account which never changes at all.

The term "other deposits" conceals a complicated account under a simple name, for it includes not only the deposits of private traders, of corporations and of foreign governments, but also the surplus money of the London bankers, and of many country banks. It is the bankers' balances which constitute the most important and most interesting element of the "other deposits," and at one time the amount of these balances was shown separately, in a return periodically made to Government. This return has been discontinued since 1877, but the desirability of its renewal in some form or other has often been mooted. In the absence of express information it is usual to assume that the principal changes in the amount of the "other deposits" are caused by changes in the bankers' balances, and it therefore becomes necessary to examine how these balances are affected by the changes of the money market. Firstly, then, as to the creation of a deposit with the Bank of England. If A wishes to open an account at the Bank, he may do so by paying in notes or gold or by giving in a cheque payable to himself. In any case A will then be able to say that so much of the "other deposits" belongs to him, but, so far as the money market is concerned, there may be a vital difference according as A's cheque is drawn against the account of a private trader or against the account of Government. Suppose that A's cheque is one for £100, given to him in the course of his business, and drawn upon Lloyd's bank. The effect of sending this cheque to the Bank of England will be to increase A's account by £100, and to decrease the balance of Lloyd's bank by a similar sum. The total amount of "other deposits" will be unaltered. If, however, A is, *e.g.*, a permanent official in some Government office, and if he opens an account at the Bank of England by sending there one of his monthly salary cheques, the effect of this will be to increase A's account by (say) £100, and to decrease "public deposits" by a similar sum. The amount of "other deposits" will, therefore, be increased by £100. "Other deposits" represent the total sum which the money market can at any moment claim from the Bank, and which the Bank would be bound to pay in notes or gold if required. The joint-stock bankers treat their balances with the Bank of England as being equivalent to gold, and include such balances in the basis of "cash in hand and at the Bank of England" upon which they rest their superstructure of loans. Any operation, therefore, which increases the amount of "other deposits" is of great importance

to the money market, inasmuch as it means that more
loans can be given. If, for instance, bankers may be
supposed to keep a proportion of cash to liabilities of
15 per cent., then an increase of the "other deposits"
by £100 will mean that additional credit to the extent
of about £700 will be available. It is important to
notice that such an increase of "other deposits" may be
brought about, as explained above, by a transference
of money from "public deposits," and that, conversely,
a decrease of "other deposits" may occur through
the transference of money to "public deposits." The
most marked example of such a transference occurs
during the first quarter of every year when, owing
to the collection of the assessed taxes, the "public
deposits" are largely increased at the expense of the
"other deposits." The joint-stock bankers, at such a
time, in order to maintain their proper proportion of
cash to liabilities, call in some of the loans which they
have made to bill-brokers, and these bill-brokers are
obliged to face the disagreeable necessity of applying
to the Bank of England for accommodation, and of
paying bank rate for the loans so obtained. This
brings to our notice another method by which "other
deposits" may be increased ; namely, by the creation
of book credits. The Bank of England, when applied
to for a loan, gives to the applicant a book credit
against which he may draw cheques ; and thus the
amount of "other deposits" is increased. Thus if,

during the month of February, the joint-stock bankers
call in loans to the amount of £1,000,000, the bill-
brokers who are thus deprived of their raw material,
go to the discount office of the Bank of England and
apply for loans to a similar amount. When these
applications are granted, "other deposits" will show
an increase of £1,000,000. A similar state of affairs
may be observed at those times of uncertainty when
bankers try to strengthen their position by increasing
their proportion of cash to liabilities. This they do
by calling in loans, and the persons thus deprived of
their money are compelled to have recourse to the
Bank of England. Thus, at a time of panic, the
"other deposits" will increase in precisely the same
way as they do at a time when there is merely a
seasonable withdrawal of credit without any dis-
placement of confidence.

Just as the item "other deposits" may be increased
by the loans of the Bank to bill-brokers or others
upon the security of bills of exchange, so it may be
decreased by what is practically the borrowing of the
Bank from the market upon the security of consols.
When the directors think that the market rate of
discount is too low, owing to the amount of "other
deposits," they sometimes take steps to reduce this
amount by a temporary sale of a portion of their
"public" or "other" securities. If the Bank, for
instance, sells £100,000 consols, the buyers will pay

for them with cheques upon various banks. The accounts of these banks with the Bank of England will be debited with the amounts of the cheques, and "other deposits" will thus be decreased by £100,000. The item "public securities" will, of course, be decreased by a similar amount.

A third manner in which "other deposits" may be increased or decreased is by changes in the demand for coin. When the volume of trade shrinks, the demand for coin will be lessened, and coin will accumulate in the coffers of the country and of the London bankers. These bankers, as already explained, do not keep the whole of their reserve in their own hands, but send a part of their spare supplies to the Bank of England. Eventually, therefore, the superfluous coin of the country collects at the Bank of England, is there credited to the bankers who have sent it, and so swells the amount of "other deposits."

A fourth cause of changes in the amount of "other deposits" is found in the exports and imports of gold. An importer of gold, unless he can get more favourable terms from foreign buyers, will bring his gold to the Bank of England, which is always ready to buy. Having arranged to sell his gold to the Bank, the importer will probably ask for payment in notes, and will pay these notes in to his account at (say) Lloyd's bank. But in consequence of this transaction Lloyd's bank will have an excess of notes, and will, therefore, return them to the Bank of England, where they will be credited to the account of Lloyd's bank, and will thus go to swell "other deposits." Conversely, a trader who buys gold from the Bank of England will probably pay for it by means of a cheque on some joint-stock bank. This cheque will be set off against the credit standing to the account of the bank on the books of the Bank of England, and "other deposits" will, to that extent, be decreased.

We have thus seen that changes in the amount of "other deposits" may occur, firstly, owing to changes in the amount of "public deposits"; secondly, owing to an increase or decrease of book credits; thirdly, owing to a contraction or expansion of the circulating medium; fourthly, owing to international demands for gold.

The next item in the return—"seven day and other bills"—is always of an insignificant amount. It includes "bank post bills," *i.e.* a species of promissory note, made by the Bank, and payable at seven days' sight.

On the assets side of the balance-sheet the first entry is "Government securities." This covers the Bank's holdings of British Government stocks, of Treasury bills, of Exchequer bonds, and of deficiency bills; these last being the security given by Government to cover temporary advances made by the Bank. Such advances are usually required at the end of the quarter, if the Government balance is insufficient to meet the dividend and other payments which then become due. Again, at a time when gold is flowing out of the country, a decrease of "Government securities" indicates, as has already been explained, that the Bank is borrowing from the market in order to tighten up the outside rate of discount.

"Other securities" includes all advances, other than advances to the British Government, whether made on the security of gilt-edged securities or in discount of bills. It includes also the investments of the Bank in securities other than those of the British Government, and also some miscellaneous assets, such as the value of the branch premises. In a return formerly made to Parliament the amounts of loans and discounts were stated separately; but this return was discontinued in 1875, so that the business of the Bank is now carried on in comparative obscurity. It is said, however, that the principal business of the Bank with borrowers lies in the direction of short loans upon the security of gilt-edged investments, and that it discounts few bills except at times when the joint-stock banks refuse to lend. Thus, during the first quarter of the year, when the "other deposits" tend to decrease owing to the collection of taxes, the joint-stock banks have to call in some of their loans. The persons who are deprived of accommodation are driven to apply to the only institution which will lend at such a time, namely, the Bank of England, thus causing an increase of "other securities." Similarly, in times of panic, the only place where loans can be obtained is the Bank of England, and the rise in the amount of " other securities " is then enormous. During the crisis of 1866 "other securities" increased by £10,000,000 in seven days ; and in 1890, during the Baring difficulties, by £7,000,000 in seven days. So long, however, as the Bank retains the confidence of the community, the majority of borrowers, even in the worst of panics, do not take advantage of their loan by asking for cash on the spot. They prefer to leave their money in the keeping of the Bank, and by so doing cause that increase of "other deposits" which is characteristic of periods of uneasiness.

The next two items—"notes" and "gold and silver coins"—are frequently grouped together under the title of "reserve." It is the practice of the banking department, as has already been explained, to keep only such stock of gold as is needed for the business of the day, and to hand over the remainder to the issue department in exchange for notes. The reserve, therefore, though consisting apparently to a large extent of notes, is in reality a reserve of gold, for the banking department can at any moment take back these notes to the issue department, and change them for gold. It has been shown how the strength of a banker's position may be deduced from the proportion which his "cash in hand and at the Bank of England" bears to his "deposits of customers." In the case of the Bank of England a similar deduction may be made from the proportion which the "reserve" bears to the sum of the "public" and "other" deposits ; for these "deposits" represent the sum which the Bank of England might be called upon to pay in gold, and the "reserve" represents the sum which it could so pay. It would, however, give a more truthful representation of the Bank's position if the proportion of the "reserve" to "other deposits" only were considered. Firstly, because the variations of "public deposits" are seasonal in their nature, and can be foreseen with comparative certainty. Secondly, because the "public deposits" are not made the basis of a superstructure of credit as are the "other deposits."

It is usual, as a matter of convenience, to talk of the "other deposits" as if they consisted entirely of bankers' balances. As a matter of fact, it is probable that bankers' balances amount to somewhat less than one-half of the total ; but so long as this fact is kept in mind it can do little harm to speak of the item "other deposits" as if it were synonymous with bankers' balances. It is important to remember that the sum of gold and notes held by the Bank of England is a reserve against "other deposits" which themselves form part of the reserve held by bankers against their "deposits of customers." The customers' deposits are generally stated at about £1,000,000,000. Against this vast sum the bankers hold, perhaps, £30,000,000[1] in their own vaults, and about £20,000,000 as "other deposits" with the Bank of England. Since the bankers are liable to pay a large part of this £1,000,000,000 in gold on demand it is obvious that if only a fraction of their customers take fright, and ask for gold, the whole reserve of gold might be drained away. Moreover, since the banks, under such circumstances, would meet the first demands by drawing gold from the Bank of England before beginning to trench upon their own reserves, it becomes clear that the Bank of England will have to bear the main burden of a panic. The banks, at such a time,

[1] Some years ago it was usually stated that the joint stock banks kept no gold beyond that required for the business of the day, and sent the remainder to the Bank of England. Sir F. Schuster, in a paper—"The Bank of England and the State"—read at Manchester University in 1905, stated that "It is very probable that the cash reserves of many bankers are not now represented entirely by their balances in the Bank of England, or by what is generally described as their till money; but that they do hold actual cash reserves not used in their daily business." There is only one bank—The Union of London and Smith's—which states these amounts separately. On Dec. 31, 1909 this bank had £3,262,166 in hand, and £2,962,474 at the Bank of England.

try to save themselves by calling in their loans to
brokers, discount houses, and others. The brokers
who have, of course, already used in buying bills the
money lent to them, cannot repay the banks unless
they can find some other lender. They are, therefore,
compelled to go to the Bank of England to obtain
money, and the Bank has to accommodate them as
far as possible in order to prevent serious disaster.
It may finally become evident that the notes in the
reserve must soon be exhausted. Under the provisions of the Act of 1844 the Bank is not allowed to
issue notes, beyond the amount of the fiduciary issue,
except against gold ; an exception which, at such a
time, is of no use whatever. Three times since the
year 1844 have the affairs of the Bank reached this
acute phase, and on each occasion the Government
of the day authorised the directors to act in contra-
vention of the Act by issuing *against securities* such
notes as might be required. On two occasions, *i.e.* in
1847 and 1866, the mere knowledge that the Bank
had power to issue notes was sufficient to check the
panic, the drain upon the reserve ceased, and finally
there was no occasion to issue the illegal notes. In
1857, however, the directors issued notes against
securities to the extent of £2,000,000 in excess of the
legal fiduciary issue. The experience of these three
crises would seem to show that when a period of
uneasiness has ripened into a panic, and people are

beginning to hoard gold and notes, the best remedy
is a liberal supply of more notes. On this ground it
has frequently been suggested that England should
follow the example of Germany, and that the Bank
of England should be allowed to issue notes against
securities to any amount, and at any time, provided
that a tax of (say) 5 per cent. be paid by the Bank to
Government upon the amount of the issue beyond a
certain fixed sum. Thus there would be none of the
mental strain which inevitably occurs under the
present law while men are waiting for the suspension
of the Bank Act, and, at the same time, owing to the
operation of the tax, the Bank would be under an
inducement to reduce its fiduciary issue to the un-
taxed limit as soon as possible.

The effect of a panic upon the position of the
Bank may be analysed as follows :—Firstly, there is
the effect due to the efforts of the other banks to
strengthen their position. Secondly, there is the
effect due to the efforts of the general public to
obtain gold and notes. We can isolate the first effect
by supposing that the feeling of uneasiness is confined
to the banks. These banks, by calling in loans, will
compel bill-brokers and others to bring securities to
the Bank of England, and so to obtain a credit on its
books. Thus "other securities" and "other deposits"
will be increased. The brokers will then repay the
banks by means of cheques on the Bank of England.

So long as the banks are willing to take repayment of their debts in the shape of a credit on the books of the Bank of England, and so long as the Bank of England is willing to give such credits there need be no demand for gold. But supposing that, as in America, there were no central institution prepared to lend during periods of uneasiness, and with which the other banks kept reserves, then, when the banks become alarmed and call in their loans, the borrowers will be unable to get credit elsewhere, and will be obliged to pay, if, indeed, they can pay at all, in gold. There will be an immediate demand for gold, some of the borrowers, doubtless, will be unable to obtain it, and a general panic is almost inevitable. Thus, in the absence of a central bank, any alarm felt by the banks tends to create alarm amongst the public. The experience gained during the American crisis of 1907 is strongly in favour of the existence of such a central institution as tending to allay the progress of an incipient crisis by staving off, for a time at any rate, the cry for gold. It is important, however, to notice that in order to fulfil this function the central bank must have such faith in its own stability that it will lend freely at a time of acute panic, and it must be so trusted by other banks that they are prepared to accept a credit on its books as equivalent to gold. It is probable that no central bank would have the necessary confidence or pres-

tige unless it were backed by the credit of the
State[1].

The second effect of a panic upon the position of
the Bank of England, namely, the effort of the public
to obtain gold and notes, is a more serious matter.
When the customers of the banks begin to ask for
gold or notes it is inevitable that the reserve of the
Bank of England will be drawn upon, and the only
remedy for the demand is to supply gold or its
equivalent. Here again the usefulness becomes apparent of a central bank which has the confidence of
the public sufficiently to enable its notes to be taken
freely in times of suspicion. Once the confidence of
the public in the convertibility of the note is shaken
no amount of note issue will stave off a demand for
gold. It is, therefore, advisable that at ordinary
times the note issue should be backed by an adequate
and well-advertised store of gold, and, if possible, by
the credit of the State as well.

Having considered the effects of an internal drain
of gold, we must now describe the effects of an
external drain. Such a drain may arise owing to
the operation of two causes which may sometimes
act simultaneously. Firstly, an undue expansion of
credit may raise prices and cause gold to flow out of
the country. Secondly, a sudden contraction of credit

[1] The Bank of England has the moral, if not the legal, support of
the State.

in another country may cause a flow of gold from this country to fill up the gap caused by the destruction of credit. In either case an external, like an internal, drain of gold immediately makes itself visible in the form of a diminution of the reserve of the Bank of England. But since notes are of no use for export, it is absolutely necessary for the Bank to take forcible steps to prevent an undue depletion of the reserve. In the chapter on the foreign exchanges we have explained how gold tends to run out of a country to make up for a deficiency in the value of the exports as compared with the value of the imports of that country, how the expense of shipping gold may be avoided by encouraging foreigners to take bills instead, and how the sale of bills may be increased by making them cheap, that is, by raising the rate of discount. The remedy for an external drain of gold, therefore, lies in the raising of the rate of discount. But herein lies the difficulty ; for the evil effects of an outflow of gold are felt mainly by one body, *i.e.* the Bank of England, whereas the power of applying the remedy lies largely in the hands of other bodies, *i.e.* the joint-stock banks, and it is obvious that the joint-stock banks may be unwilling to apply a remedy which, at first sight, is rather to the benefit of their rival than of themselves. It is true that the Bank of England can always raise its own rate of discount, but this will be useless if the joint-stock banks continue to discount bills freely at a lower rate. The rate of discount fixed by the Bank of England can only be effective when the supply of money in the outside market is not sufficient for the supply of bills, *i.e.* when the supply of bills is greater than the joint-stock banks care to buy. In such case some borrowers must have recourse to the Bank of England, and must pay bank rate for their money. This, of course, will tend to raise the outside discount rate to a similar level, and to put a stop to the outflow of gold. In cases where the joint-stock banks are discounting so freely that a rise in the bank rate has no effect, it is the practice of the Bank, as has already been explained, to sell consols, and so to deprive the market of some of its superabundant supply of money[1]; a device which usually has the desired effect.

In connection with the subject of an external drain of gold, it is important to notice that accepting houses, by converting bills drawn on England into acceptable securities, and bill-brokers, by discounting such bills, are in a position to give to foreigners the power to draw upon the Bank's reserve. If *A*, resident in Paris, wishes to obtain gold from England, he may do so by drawing a bill on London, by paying

[1] Of late years the Bank of England has given up this indirect method of reducing outside supplies, and has taken to borrowing directly from the clearing bankers.

a reputable firm to give to the bill the hall-mark of
their name, and finally by discounting the bill with
a bill-broker or discount house. By virtue of the
cheque given to him by the bill-broker, A will then
be able to draw gold from the bank upon which the
cheque is drawn, and this bank, in its turn, will
replenish its coffers by drawing out in gold or notes
a portion of its balance with the Bank of England.
Thus the signature of the accepting house upon the
bill, combined with the signature of the bill-broker
upon the cheque, amounts almost to an order to
the Bank of England to pay out gold. By being
too lavish in their acceptances or their discounts of
bills held by foreigners, the accepting houses and
bill-brokers may, in certain circumstances, cause a
serious outflow of gold, and this quite apart from any
inflation of prices. The most famous example of an
outflow of gold brought about in this way was due
not to the action of private individuals but to the
exigencies of a great war. In order to facilitate the
raising of funds for the purpose of subsidising the
Continental allies of England, Pitt, in 1793, procured
the passage of an Act enabling the directors of the
Bank of England to lend money to Government
without the consent of Parliament, a procedure which
had been forbidden by the first Bank Act in 1695.
Armed with the powers conferred by the new Act,
the Prime Minister was enabled to pay the foreign

subsidies by the simple expedient of accepting bills drawn upon him from the Continent and made payable at the Bank of England. In the three years 1793–1795 the foreign subsidies amounted to nine millions and a half. Owing to the operations of the holders of these bills on England the foreign exchanges became very adverse, and metal flowed rapidly out of the country. Finally, in 1797, an internal panic arose, and the Bank, being unable, owing to its reduced reserve, to meet the demand for gold, was compelled to suspend cash payments. Although accepting houses and bill-brokers were not to blame for the outflow of gold during these years, yet their parts were played by the Government and the Bank of England respectively, and the underlying principle is the same. In justice to the directors of the Bank of England, it is necessary to add that they persistently pointed out to the Prime Minister the extreme danger involved in any extension of his, already vast, liabilities, although they did not go so far as to refuse to honour any of the acceptances of the Government which were presented for payment at the Bank.

CHAPTER X

Owing to its position as the only free market for gold the London money market is very subject to fluctuations. This rate of discount may be well illustrated with reference to our hydraulic model. England may there be represented by a central cylinder which is connected with many other cylinders, representing other gold-using countries. But these other cylinders must be supposed to have no connecting tubes amongst themselves. That is, everyone of them is dependent upon England alone to supply any deficiency or to drain off any excess of water. If, owing to the sudden collapse of the credit bag, there arises in any cylinder a deficiency of water this deficiency will be first felt in the cylinder representing England, and with great severity. From the English cylinder it will make its influence felt in a much less degree in all the other cylinders. That is to say, a collapse of credit in any country will lead to a sudden demand for gold which will be felt very keenly in England, and to a less extent in all other countries.

Thus, during the American crisis of 1907, nearly £25,000,000 in gold was shipped to New York. The greater part of this sum came direct from London, but the Bank of England, by raising its rate of discount, drew gold from seventeen other countries, and to the amount of more than £15,000,000. Similarly a violent contraction of trade in any country (if unaccompanied by a concomitant contraction of credit) will cause an overflow of gold which will first collect in the English market, and then flow gradually to other gold-using countries.

The extreme susceptibility of the English money market to foreign demands for gold has given occasion for criticisms which may be placed under two heads. Firstly, it is said that the store of gold held in England, and available to meet abnormal demands, is so small that it might be brought to a dangerously low level, or even be altogether exhausted, before effective measures could be taken to stop the drain or to replenish the store of gold from other sources. Secondly, it is said that a small reserve of gold necessitates frequent and violent changes in the rate of discount, and that such changes are not only a hindrance to internal trade, but also a menace to the international supremacy of the London money market. An addition to existing gold reserves is therefore advocated on the ground that it would be an insurance against financial disaster, and also on the ground that it would enable the English money market to meet sudden demands for gold with less frequent and less violent changes in the rate of discount.

As a preliminary to the discussions of these questions it is necessary to obtain a clear idea of the meaning of the term "gold reserves," more especially because this term has been used in different senses by different writers, and sometimes even by the same writer, without any note of warning. The term "gold reserve" has been applied (1) to the store of gold, apart from till-money, held by banks other than the Bank of England; (2) to the gold and notes held by the banking department of the Bank of England; (3) to the gold held by the issue department of the Bank of England; (4) to a proposed store of gold (often spoken of as a "secondary reserve") to which the Government as well as the banks should contribute, and which should be held by some central authority, such as the Bank of England, for use at times of emergency; (5) to a proposed store of gold to be accumulated by the Government to sustain the credit of the nation, and to meet sudden demands in case of war or other emergency. This is sometimes described as a "national reserve."

Whatever the meaning of the term, however, the proposals to increase our gold reserves have one main object in view, namely, to strengthen the gold foundation upon which such a heavy superstructure of credit is based. The case of a country which has an inadequate store of gold may be represented on our hydraulic model by a cylinder the interior of which is mainly occupied by a much inflated credit bag, and which consequently contains very little water. If this cylinder were to become suddenly thinner, the little water which it contained might be driven out altogether before any remedial measures could be adopted. Such a danger might be obviated by permanently reducing the size of the credit bag as compared with the volume of the cylinder, and so drawing in an increased quantity of water. But without requiring any reduction of the proportion which the volume of the credit bag bears to the volume of the cylinder, the contingency of a sudden outflow of water may be provided against by establishing a small store of water *outside* the cylinder, but in such a position that it may be pumped into the cylinder whenever occasion may require, and may be taken out again when the crisis is over. Similarly, the financial security of a gold-using country may be assured to some extent (1) by reducing the proportion which the volume of credit bears to the reserve of gold held by the bankers, or (2) by establishing a store of gold which shall be kept outside the ordinary operations of banking, and shall not be brought into use except in times of emergency.

The first principle applies to an increase of "gold reserves" in the first three of the five meanings outlined above. The second principle is involved in the establishment of gold reserves in the fourth and fifth of these meanings.

We shall now proceed to examine in greater detail the chief proposals which have been made for an increase of our gold reserves.

Reserves held by banks other than the Bank of England.

In a previous chapter it has been explained that the proportion of "cash" to "customers' deposits" in the balance-sheet of a bank is usually taken as the measure of its stability. But "customers' deposits," being largely made up of book credits on which the bank draws interest, is a good measure of the bank's earning power. A bank manager, therefore, is impelled on the one hand by the force of public opinion, to keep the ratio of "cash" to "customers' deposits" as large as possible, whilst, on the other hand, he is impelled by the desire for gain, to increase deposits without any regard to the amount of cash. It has therefore been proposed to strengthen the force of public opinion at the expense of the desire for gain (and so to diminish the volume of credit) by inducing or compelling the larger banks to make monthly statements showing their *average*[1] position throughout the month, and giving clear details as to the amount of gold and notes held by them, and of their balance with the Bank of England; the smaller banks to publish quarterly statements of a similar kind. If, as is generally assumed to be the case, the immediate effect of greater publicity were to be an increase in the ratio of cash to deposits the following train of events would ensue. Since cash could not be suddenly increased deposits must have decreased, and this implies a contraction of credit and a rise in the rate of discount. Gold would therefore flow in from other countries, and the banks would create credits against it until the rate of discount of the English money market attained equilibrium with the rates of discount of other countries.

Granted that an increase of publicity will be followed by an increase in the stock of gold held by the banks, the question arises as to whether the banks shall keep this gold in their own vaults or deposit it with the Bank of England. Against the first course it has been urged that in times of panic each bank hugs its own store of gold so as to be prepared for emergencies, whereas the best way of averting a panic is to lend freely. The only institution which lends freely at a time of panic is the Bank

[1] Accounts giving the position of a bank on one day only are obviously susceptible of manipulation.

of England. Therefore it is better that gold should
be in the vaults of the Bank of England than in those
of some other bank. On the other hand, the argu-
ments of those who maintain that all spare gold
should be deposited with the Bank of England are
open to two objections. Firstly, all gold deposited
with the Bank of England is made the basis of *two*
systems of credit. For every £10 deposited with the
Bank of England the depositing bank has lent (say)
£70, and the Bank of England will lend (say) £25.
The total amount of credit created is £95, whereas,
if the gold had been kept by the bank which
owned it, the total amount of credit created there-
against would have been only £70. Secondly,
there is the insuperable objection that the joint
stock banks by depositing a larger amount of gold
with the Bank of England would be benefiting "a
rival establishment whose competition they already
feel with increasing severity." This conflict between
the desire of the public for a central reserve, and the
dislike of the banks for any scheme which would
unduly benefit a rival has led to the conception of a
"secondary reserve"; a conception which will be
amplified in a subsequent section.

Before leaving the subject of reserves held by
banks other than the Bank of England, it will be
advisable to mention briefly the American legislation
designed in order to compel the national banks to

keep an adequate reserve. The gist of this legislation is that such banks must keep a fixed proportion (in some cases 15 per cent., in others 25 per cent.) of gold to deposits. This plan is subject to the disadvantage that if a fit of suspicion seizes the commercial world at a time when the reserves of the banks are near their minimum, the banks are unable to lend freely unless they are prepared to break the law, and they are therefore practically debarred from doing anything to stave off the incipient panic.

The "Reserve" of the Bank of England.

The proportion which the reserve bears to the total of "public" and "other deposits" varies from 35 to 55 per cent.; a much higher proportion than that kept by the principal joint-stock banks. The Bank of England, of course, pays no interest on deposits, and therefore is able with profit to keep a larger reserve than banks which do pay interest. The question of the mere amount of the reserve, however, is not separable from the question of discount rates. A firm and judicious manipulation of the bank rate combined, if necessary, with borrowings in the open market is just as important as, and in fact, necessary to, the preservation of a large reserve. The efficacy of this device, however, depends entirely upon the confidence placed by foreign

financiers in the stability of English conditions. A
high rate of discount will only attract gold from
abroad, insomuch as it induces foreigners to invest
their money in bills on England, and bills on England
will not be attractive as investments if there is any
likelihood of their failing to be met upon maturity.
Thus during the crisis of 1866 uneasiness on the
Continent with regard to the position of the Bank of
England had reached such a pitch, that large quantities of long dated bills on England were sent over to
be discounted at any rate which could be got and the
proceeds taken away in gold. Even while the rate
of discount was 10 per cent. in England and 4 per
cent. in France, gold continued to flow out of the
country. We see, therefore, that under certain
circumstances a rise in the bank rate will be inoperative, and in such a case the actual volume of
the reserve will be the principal consideration.

Besides the holding of an adequate reserve, and
a wise use of the bank rate the Bank of England has,
upon special occasions, made use of other means to
maintain its position. The first of these occasions
was in 1839 when the Bank had allowed its stock of
bullion to become seriously depleted. On the 16th
of July this stock had fallen below £3,000,000. " The
directors at last woke to the fact that the Bank was
rapidly drifting into bankruptcy. On the 13th of
July they gave notice that they would be ready to

receive tenders for the purchases of some terminable
annuities, but the minimum they fixed was so high
that no sale took place....The Bank [had also] sold
public securities to the amount of £760,000, and [had]
authorised bills upon Paris to be drawn to its account
to the amount of £600,000.   These measures had the
effect for a short time of arresting the drain.   But
when these bills came to maturity the Bank was in
no better position to meet them, and it then became
necessary to create a larger credit in Paris to meet
the first.   The position of the Bank was, of course,
well known to all the foreign dealers in exchange,
and in June it was generally expected abroad that
the Bank could not maintain payments in specie.
In consequence of this, all long dated bills upon this
country were sent over for immediate realisation,
and the values withdrawn as speedily as possible.
To counteract this drain as well as to meet the
payments of the first credit which had been created
on behalf of the Bank, it was obliged, in July, to
organise a measure of a much larger nature.   Messrs
Baring entered into an agreement with twelve of the
leading bankers of Paris, to draw bills upon them to
the amount of upwards of £2,000,000....An operation
of a similar nature, to the amount of £900,000, was
organised with Hamburg.   As soon as any bill was
drawn on account of one of these operations, the
Bank transferred an equal amount of the annuities

it had offered for sale in July to two trustees, one for the drawers and one for the acceptor. Out of this second credit the bills which fell due from the creation of the first credit were paid. This measure had the effect of gradually arresting the drain of bullion[1]."

Curiously enough the second occasion upon which the Bank of England was obliged to have recourse to extraordinary measures in order to meet its obligations is also connected with the name of Baring, but in 1890 it was the difficulties of Messrs Baring, not of the Bank of England, which brought about the crisis. It is not necessary to give here details of the panic of that year. We need only state that a strong demand for gold arose in the city, and that the Bank was obliged to import gold to the value of £4,500,000, of which £3,000,000 was borrowed from the Bank of France and £1,500,000 from the Bank of Russia. From a consideration of these two examples, it becomes obvious that the sale of bills on gold standard countries and the borrowing of gold from other central banks must be included amongst the resources of the Bank of England which are available to protect its reserve.

It is sometimes objected that the "reserve," apart from its actual amount, is composed for the most part of notes, and that of these notes a certain

[1] H. D. Macleod, *Theory and Practice of Banking*, Vol. II, p. 144.

proportion is issued against securities, and is therefore not equivalent to gold. This objection leads us to the consideration of the store of gold held by the issue department.

Gold held by the Issue Department.

In the specimen bank return given in Chapter IX the gross issue of notes is shown as £52,500,395, and of this amount nearly 18½ millions or about 35 per cent. is backed by securities. The fiduciary issue, it will be remembered, was originally £14,000,000 (of which £11,015,100 was issued against a book debt due from the Government to the Bank of England), and has increased to its present amount through the taking over of the lapsed issues of other banks. The profits on this extra 4½ millions of fiduciary issue go to the State.

It has often been contended that the extent of the fiduciary issue is a weak spot in the English currency system, and that it should be reduced. Several schemes have been proposed having this object in view, and of these the best known is Lord Goschen's proposal of 1891 for the issue of £1 notes in England. £1 notes have a wide circulation in Scotland and Ireland, but in England their use has been forbidden since the Act of 1826. Lord Goschen proposed to repeal this Act and to give authority to

the Bank of England to issue £1 notes, four-fifths
against gold and one-fifth against securities, such
authority not to commence unless the stock of gold
in the issue department was at or above £21,500,000.
This sum was in 1890 the average amount of gold
held by the issue department, and would at the
present day be represented by a sum of about
£35,000,000. The effect of such a scheme may be
seen by considering an imaginary return of the issue
department after 25 millions of £1 notes had been
taken into circulation. If we suppose the issue of
£5 notes to be £50,000,000, the return before the
issue of £1 notes would appear as follows:

Liabilities	£	Assets	£
Notes issued	50,000,000	Government debt	11,015,100
		Other securities	7,434,900
		Gold	31,550,000
	£50,000,000		£50,000,000

showing a ratio of gold to notes of about 64 per cent.
After the issue of £1 notes it would appear as follows:

Liabilities	£	Assets	£
Notes issued	75,000,000	Government debt	11,015,100
		Other securities	12,434,900
		Gold	51,550,000
	£75,000,000		£75,000,000

showing a ratio of gold to notes of about 69 per cent.
Thus the proportionate amount of the fiduciary issue

would be considerably reduced, and the position of the issue department would be to that extent strengthened. It was objected to Lord Goschen's scheme that under its operation notes to the value of (say) £25,000,000 would be put into circulation, while gold to the value of £20,000,000 would be taken out of circulation, and that therefore, if the currency requirements of the people remained the same, gold to the value of £5,000,000 would be driven out of the country. To this Lord Goschen replied that twenty millions of gold in the Bank of England was much more valuable as a reserve than twenty-five millions in the pockets of the people.

Lord Goschen further proposed that if the issue of £1 notes was successful, the Bank of England, armed with its increased store of gold, might be given power in times of internal crisis, at a given rate of interest, to issue notes irrespective of the bullion obligation. "That rate of interest must be neither so high as to make the whole operation inoperative nor so low as to encourage people to speculate up to it in the certainty that they would be able at a reasonable rate of interest to carry through their obligations." The test of the necessity for an emergency issue was to be the reduction of the stock of gold held by the Bank of England to a certain level. When the stock of gold had fallen to this level, the power to issue notes without a backing

of gold was to come into operation, provided the
exchanges were favourable.

Another scheme for the reduction of the fiduciary
issue consists in the repayment by the Government
of its debt to the Bank. Funds for this purpose
could be provided by means of additional taxation
or, more reasonably, from the Sinking Fund. In
either case, as the result of such operation, "public
deposits" would be greater by eleven millions than
they would otherwise have been. The repayment of
the debt could then be accomplished by striking off
this sum from the credit of the Government on the
books of the Bank of England, and the banking
department could then hand over notes to the value
of £11,015,100 to the issue department for cancella-
tion. If this scheme were adopted the return of the
issue department would, on the basis of existing
averages, be somewhat as follows:

Liabilities	£	Assets	£
Notes issued	50,000,000	Securities	7,434,900
		Gold ...	42,565,100
	£50,000,000		£50,000,000

showing a ratio of gold to notes of about 85 per cent.
If the Bank was still empowered to issue notes against
securities to the amount of eighteen-and-a-half
millions, as before, it would, in times of panic be

able to make an emergency issue without any breach of the law.

It should be noted that the benefit of an increased stock of gold in the issue department would be confined almost entirely to cases of an internal drain of gold, when an emergency issue of notes is required or when public confidence in the convertibility of the note is shaken. An external drain takes the form of a withdrawal of notes from the banking department and the encashment of these notes at the issue department. As the reserve of the banking department rarely amounts to 30 millions, whilst the gold in the issue department rarely falls below 35 millions, it is obvious that the banking department is the vulnerable point of the system in the case of an external drain of gold.

The Secondary Reserve.

Up to this point we have treated of schemes which involve merely the reduction of the proportion of credit to reserve. The gist of the principle of a secondary reserve is that some quantity of gold shall be taken out of the market altogether, and shall not be used as a basis of credit at all. The details of the scheme, however, have taken various forms. The two main points of difference are: Who shall bear the cost of the reserve? Where shall the reserve be

kept, and who shall have control over it? It is
generally admitted, even by bankers themselves, that
the banks should bear some part of the burden of
a secondary reserve. The Government also, it has
been pointed out, inasmuch as it benefits by the
creation of cheap credit, ought to give some help.
Another point made against the Government in this
connection is that no reserve of gold is kept against
the deposits of the Post Office and Trustee Savings
Banks. These deposits amount to more than 200
millions, and the only reserve consists of consols to
about one-third of that amount. It has been urged
that in the case of wars or labour troubles a run
upon the savings banks might result, and that this,
in the absence of any gold reserve, would necessitate
the sale of consols, and would probably create a very
serious situation in the money market. But the
general consensus of opinion would seem to be that
the contribution of the Government should take the
form, not of a gift of gold to a secondary reserve, but
of the repayment of the debt which it owes to the
Bank of England, and of the consequent reduction of
the fiduciary issue. Under existing arrangements
this would involve a loss by the Government of the
profits on $4\frac{1}{2}$ millions, and by the Bank of the
profits on $6\frac{1}{2}$ millions, of fiduciary issue; thus
throwing an unfair share of the burden on the Bank.
But the burden could, of course, be allotted in any

proportions which it was thought just to arrange. If, then, the cost of reducing the fiduciary issue is considered to have discharged the obligations of the Government and the Bank of England towards the maintenance of the national credit, the entire burden of the secondary reserve must be borne by the other banks.

As to the allocation and control of the secondary reserve we will quote two well-known schemes. Firstly, the suggestion of Sir Felix Schuster[1], that the reserve should be kept at the Bank of England under the control of a small permanent committee, to be formed of representatives of the bankers, acting with the Bank of England; that without the committee's sanction the special reserve should never be used, and such sanction should be given only in circumstances of exceptional urgency.

Secondly, we have a somewhat inchoate scheme outlined in the Report of the Gold Reserves Commitee of the London Chamber of Commerce, issued in July 1909. The terms of this resolution are as follows: "That the bullion department of the Bank of England affords a means by its enlargement for the aggregation of gold reserves held by others than the Government of India, viz.:

(a) The banks of the United Kingdom, including

---

[1] Paper read before the Institute of Bankers, December 1906.

the Bank of England, in respect of such gold held against their liabilities in excess of till money as any of them may elect to deposit in the bullion department.

(b) Scotch and Irish banks in respect of all or any portion of the extra gold held by them against excess issue under the Act of 1845[1].

(c) The National Debt Commissioners and the Postmaster-General in respect of the gold which the committee recommend should be held against the liabilities of trustee savings banks and post office savings banks respectively."

Both these schemes, it will be noticed, provide for the location of the secondary reserve at the Bank of England; but they differ on the subject of its control. The committee of the London Chamber of Commerce suggest, by implication at any rate, that each institution should retain complete control of the gold which it had chosen to deposit in the bullion department. Sir Felix Schuster, on the other hand, would place the control of the reserve in the hands of a representative committee. The latter suggestion would,

---

[1] By Statute 1845, c. 38, each of such banks was authorised to have in circulation an amount of notes whose average for four weeks was not to exceed the amount of its average issues during the year preceding May 1st, 1845, together with an equal amount to the average amount of coin held by the bank during the same four weeks. Of this coin at least three-quarters must be gold.

at first sight, appear to be the most reasonable, inasmuch as a reserve so controlled would be disposable for the common good, and would not be liable to the caprice of individual banks; but it is open to the objection that the directors of a joint-stock bank could not, consistently with the duty which they owe to their shareholders, consent to part with the exclusive control of any funds belonging to the bank. But even though it were not feasible to provide for the central control of the secondary reserve, yet the existence of a permanent committee, formed of representatives of the bankers to act with the Bank of England would be a most valuable safeguard to the English monetary system. If, for instance, it could be arranged by a representative committee that no bank should lend at a lower rate than 1 per cent. below bank rate, a link would be established between bank rate and market rate which would render unnecessary the inconvenient borrowing policy of the Bank of England, and would do away with the deluge of cheap money which at some periods encourages speculation to an undesirable extent.

The National Reserve.

The possession of a store of precious metal by the State was a prominent feature of mediaeval finance,

but with the rise of banking and the consequent
development of systematic public indebtedness the
necessity for State treasures became less pressing[1].
But while the opinion of financiers has become
adverse to the maintenance of a State treasure as a
means for defraying extraordinary expenses, it has,
of late years, advocated the accumulation of treasure
as a means of adding stability to the credit of the
State.   Even though at a time of widespread panic
or national disaster such a store of gold might be
hopelessly inadequate to meet the demands made
upon it, yet its existence might do much to ward off
such dangers.

It is necessary to distinguish between a non-
economic reserve, such as the German war chest
at Spandau, and a reserve which is in some way
connected with the ordinary liabilities of the State.
Thus in countries where the regulation of the paper
currency is undertaken by the State, the State must
maintain a reserve against the note issue.   The
Indian Government, for example, keeps about three
rupees of silver for every four rupees of notes issued.
Again, in England, the Government has incurred vast
liabilities to depositors in the post office savings
banks.   It has not, however, accumulated any store
of cash to meet their possible demands ; and this

---

[1] Bastable, *Public Finance* Bk 5, Ch. 1.

absence of any reserve has given rise to much criticism. It may be well to note, however, that a "run" upon the savings bank is a very remote contingency. The deposits, in banking phraseology, are "good lying money," and would seem to increase more rapidly during years of depression than during years of active trade. It is conceivable, indeed, that such a run might occur (1) if depositors began to doubt the continuing solvency of the Government, or (2) if owing to an invasion or to widespread labour troubles the depositing classes were compelled by privation to withdraw their deposits. In the case of a run due to panic, it is doubtful whether anything save the desperate remedy of a forced paper currency could save the situation; in the case of a run due to privation it is probable that the suspension of the Bank Act, and the payment of depositors in notes, would be an adequate and, if carefully managed, a harmless expedient. In the first case a reserve of gold would be insufficient, in the second case it would be unnecessary. But although, as an insurance against a run of savings bank depositors, a State store of gold may be out of place, yet it may be of much value in securing the confidence of foreign financiers. If, for this purpose, it were thought advisable to accumulate a State treasure in England, an obvious source of supply suggests itself in the profits from the $4\frac{1}{2}$ millions of fiduciary issue which go the State. It has been pointed out by Sir R. Giffen, that the extent of the fiduciary issue is a weak spot in the English monetary system, and that the State's share of the profits from this issue should not be treated as revenue, but should be used to build up a reserve of gold.

INDEX

9 781107 401839